Shifted!

MURDER
TRAUMA
GOD'S REDEMPTIVE
POWER

A True Story of **Love** and **Forgiveness**

Michelle Jeffries Rhodes

This book is dedicated
to

Kelvin Lee Spears,
the father of my daughter,
and a life gone too soon on purpose, for a purpose.

And
Vincent Alan Rhodes,
my husband of thirty-two years, the dad of my daughter,
and the man God intentionally placed in
my life to carry out His glorious plan.

If no one has died, it can be rectified.
—Michelle Renee Jeffries

One chance is all you need
—Jesse Owens

To every thing there is a season, and a time
to every purpose under the heaven.
—Ecclesiastes 3:1

CONTENTS

FOREWORD—VINCENT

It was the summer of 1987. I was backing out of a parking space at my apartment building.

Suddenly, BAM!

I bumped into a vehicle behind me. I stopped, hoping there was no damage to either car. Then I heard God speak to me for the first time. "You need to marry that woman," The instructions were clear: I had to marry Michelle.

Yet, I still had to ask, "God, I know you don't want me to marry that "crazy" woman?"

His answer to me was simple. "Yes."

Michelle and I were total opposites. She was loud and full of energy, and always had ideas to implement. On the other hand, I was quiet and reserved, and always weighed all options before starting any new projects.

I proceeded to marry Michelle Jeffries, and we have been married for over thirty-one years.

I have seen her take on the titanic struggle of writing this book.

She worried that telling this story would sensationalize a real tragedy in her life and obscure the real, important lessons learned in overcoming it.

But the urgency and importance of those lessons, as well as the prompting of the Holy Spirit, finally convinced Michelle that her story was needed and the book was worth completing.

Michelle, thank you for opening yourself up to me then and now to the whole world.

I love you very much.

Vincent

Me, Vincent and our children and twin grand children

FOREWORD—VAL

G od loves you unconditionally. There is nothing that you can do to make God stop loving you.

Let those words sink into your heart. There is *nothing* you can do to make God stop loving you. Oh, what a blessed assurance!

The book of Genesis teaches us that we are created in the image of God (Genesis 1:26) and that we are fearfully and wonderfully made in that sacred image (Psalms 139:14). God took time and care to form you in your mother's womb according to His glorious plan (Psalms 139:13). Once you were born, He did not leave you to go through life unguided and without direction. God thought of you even before He formed you in your mother's womb. He has plans for you (Jeremiah 29:11)!

Do we mess up? Certainly! Do we disobey God's Word? Certainly! Does God still love us? Absolutely! The story contained in this book is a great testimony of this great, unconditional love that God has for us.

The Bible says, "For God so loved the world that He gave his only begotten son, that whosoever believes in him should not perish but have everlasting life" (John 3:16). God loves you. He desires that no one perish but that all come to repentance (2 Peter 3:9). God loves you. Hallelujah!

My father used to say that God is not surprised at the things that we do. That means God wasn't surprised when Michelle got herself, to quote *The*

Sandlot, in the biggest pickle of her young life. God did not say, "Oops!" or "Uh-oh!" He knew about Michelle's dire situation before the foundations of the world; yet, He loved her. He had his eye and his hand on her the entire time. He knew He could carry her through this mess. He knew the plans He had for her on the other side. Our God is amazing!

Everyone who knows Michelle knows she has a huge personality that she is not afraid to share with the world. Her energy is infectious. To know her, you would never guess that she has been through what she has been through. But God carried her through. With his loving-kindness, He drew Michelle to Himself (Jeremiah 31:3). And what He did for her, He desires to do for you too. God loves you!

As you read Michelle's story, see yourself. Are you currently in a dire situation? God desires to help you; He is waiting with open arms for you to run to him. Even if your dire situation has already happened, does its memory or its consequences still have you bound in misery, anxiety, or depression? With God, you do not have to stay bound in negativity. God is willing and waiting to move in your life, to transform your life and your thinking, and to bring you into a glorious place of rest and peace with Him. God loves you!

Michelle shares her heart with you in this book. She shares with you the tools God used in her life to make her who she is today: an ordained elder, certified life coach, encourager, and beloved child of God filled with God's precious Holy Spirit. What He did for her, He is waiting to do for you!

If you need God to move in your life, use the tools Michelle shares with you. As you put those tools to use, invite God to move in your life, in your situation and be open to whatever He desires to do for you. God loves you!

May God richly bless you today. Be encouraged and strengthened in the power of God's might as you allow Him to work in you and to equip you in every good thing to do His will, working in you that which is pleasing in His sight, through Jesus Christ, to whom be the glory forever and ever. Amen (Hebrews 13:21).

Minister Valerie M. Whittaker, MA
Associate Minister, Eagles Nest Church
Sandusky, Ohio

A Poem by my Sister

Shared in Spoken Word

Juilee Jeffries Vanhorse

Happiness and hope...

I need and want them both
so desperately...
Aphrodisiacs..mind healers..dope.
Praying for opportunities
blessings abound
God hears my cries...
peace in Him I've found.
Salvation...devastation....manifestation....levitation..
He has me on high...
answered prayers the pinnacle of consciousness...
no worries...peace...hopeful...positive vibes.
Keep grinding my Queen..
your Lioness Heart has been seen....
your Greatness can not hide.
So they say..if it's worth having...with tears & sweat you'll pay.
That day is on its way when your legacy is revealed on full display.
Your story is being written.
God's timing is perfect...
dig deep my Queen bring those hidden gifts to the surface.
The mind is your weapon so keep it strong...
it will keep you at peace when things seem wrong.
YO...know this...it's only a test
show your belief
be different than the rest!
HOPE & HAPPINESS is dope..
no other stimulant is necessary..

pure-mind-body..& prayer to cope.
Bright future..
confidence bettin' on self …
Daniel book 10th- verse 12th Visualize & mediate—
Hope, Happiness & dreams fulfilled shall prevail.

Juilee and Me in front of Scott High School 2017

A FEW WHY'S FOR WRITING THIS BOOK?

1. To encourage you to come out of your darkness and break the shackles of your secret past.
2. To help you attain strength in your higher power.
3. To inspire you to develop consistent, streamlined schedules.
4. To teach the importance of telling the story of your life.
5. To prove some shifts in life are preventable.
6. To illustrate how human and spiritual goals can be set and reached after trauma.
7. To motivate you to never give up on love, forgiveness, or self.
8. To coach you how to create a life of peace and productivity.

The Key Conversations

Two conversations from winter 2017 were key to freeing my mind of self-imprisonment. Most importantly, I learned I had to break the shackles of my secret past, or I would be squeezed tighter and tighter. As you listen in on the following exchanges, I hope you too find encouragement to come out of the darkness and break the chains of your own past.

Sitting in church, gazing at the stained glass window located in the front of the church sanctuary, I felt tears stream down my face and neck. Although I wished I could, I couldn't stop crying. My pastor had preached "the season of uncomfortable," as he called it, and his sermon stirred up so many emotions within me. Trapped in thoughts about my past, I knew all about that season of uncomfortable.

Surrendering to another sob, I heard the Lord. "It's time," He said.

"Today is the day I want you to call Memia and Granddaddy and get permission."

Permission? I had a story I wanted to tell—the one contained in this book—but it touched more lives than just my own. What was I asking for? It was not permission to write this book, but asking for permission to tell that story, God knew, meant something deeper. It meant trying to make sure they still loved me. It meant asking for forgiveness. It meant telling the story of that tragic night more than thirty-seven years before.

Leaving church earlier that day, I knew the sermon would sit with me. I'd returned home after church but found I needed to return after making dinner for my family. Alone with God, I cried in the choir stand, thinking about what I'd been asked to do.

I looked at the clock on my phone: 2:31 p.m., December 17, 2017.

I dialed Reverend Jesse Spears—Granddaddy, as my daughter, Audrei, calls him.

I waited as the phone rang. No answer.

As I sat in the sanctuary, I looked up through the church's skylights and said, "God, you told me to call him."

God replied, "I didn't tell you to call him first. Memia comes first."

I dialed the number. The phone rang just twice, and then I heard the voice of Mrs. Lillian Spears, my daughter's grandmother, otherwise known as Memia. Hearing her voice, my crying resumed with sobs that could be heard over the phone.

I struggled to find my breath or say anything. All I could hear was Memia's voice.

"It's OK. It's OK."

I lost track of how long I'd been crying, but by the grace of God, I found my words, expressing how sorry I was for everything that had happened. I should have been the one doing the consoling.

Memia and I talked for over an hour, and she gave me permission to write the book in your hands. She didn't give me permission to write every story, but I had to include *the story.*—the one that changed the lives of so many.

Memia believed that this book would do what I set out for it to do: to help others move on from their pasts, remove masks, and live authentic lives. Now that this book is completed, I have reflected on what this book might mean for readers like you.

- This book will help you understand that you do not have to live your adult life perpetually traumatized by events from your youth.

- You can live a life of love and forgiveness, understanding that these are the two greatest tools to help you out of any darkness in your life.
- Once you manifest love and forgiveness for yourself, you will be on your way to living a life of peace and productivity.

Because Memia is such an amazing person, we ended our conversation by having Bible study over the phone.

We talked about true love and true forgiveness.

We discussed the angel Michael and how Michael was a protector.

We talked about Daniel and all the adversity he faced but still came out unscathed.

"It is not time to be silent," Memia told me that day in December. "It's time to speak and to be bold. Know that someone will be helped by our story."

Now, it may be hard, at this point, to understand why I had to call Memia and ask permission to write this book. This wasn't simply a courtesy. As you read this book, you will see how personal this story is and how Memia's unimaginable love and forgiveness made this book possible.

After our Bible study, Memia left me with three main thoughts that I would like to share with you.

1. Unconfessed sin leads to an undisciplined life and to a lack of forgiveness.
2. Forgiveness frees us from the inside.
3. Forgiveness will allow God to answer our prayers.

After I spoke with Memia, I called Granddaddy.

Granddaddy is a man of few words, and after just a few minutes of conversation, he agreed with Memia.

"This story needs to be told," he said. "I told you a very long time ago that our story needs to be on the Oprah Winfrey Show. It will show everyone that love and forgiveness can prevail. Love is unconditional, and in order for us to truly be successful in life, we must show love and have true forgiveness."

I'm grateful that I have the opportunity to write this book.

I'm even more grateful that the Spears have given me their blessings—no, not just their blessings, but their intentional, authentic love, support, and encouragement. As of writing this, Granddaddy is ninety, and Memia is eighty-five. When God wants His plan carried out, time has no age limit.

I must be intentional about explaining why I am writing this book. My hope is that whoever reads this will understand and know that no matter how unimaginably dark life may seem, and no matter how difficult the trials and tribulations, the problems, the worries, the concerns, and the obstacles, you can always have faith in God's true love and true forgiveness.

Today, I know it was my trust in God's Word that helped me come out of darkness. God's Word helped me break every shackle of my secret past and navigate the shifting in my life.

Likewise, God's Word will help you come out of darkness and into His marvelous light to create a life of peace and productivity. God's Word will help you navigate the shifting in your life. It is simple but not easy.

Lessons Learned

From the introduction, we have learned that to come out of darkness and break the shackles of a secret past, we must confess our sins to live a disciplined life. This cultivates a mindset of willing forgiveness.

Sinner's Prayer

Lord I confess that I am a sinner. I am sorry for my sins. I want to live for you. I believe that Jesus, your son, died for my sins. Today, I confess that I am turning away from living for the world. Now I live for the kingdom of God. I am saved through the blood of Jesus. I am saved!

1. Forgiveness frees us from the inside.
2. Forgiveness will allow God to answer our prayers.

To wade through the darkness of your past secrets and hurts, you must face them.

Your First Homework Assignment

Write this scripture every day for the next ninety days:

> *Thou wilt keep him in perfect peace, whose mind is stayed on thee: because he trusteth in thee.* (Isaiah 26:3)

So often our minds are focused on the problems of the world. Today, let's shift. Today, let's start creating new thoughts, a new mindset—one that will help create peace in our lives. As you continue to read this book, you will be challenged to focus on God's Word. This focus, with the right tools, has helped me sharpen my mind and bring me out of darkness. I am going to share these tools with you so you, too, can find your way.

First Tool: The Bible.

* * *

CHAPTER 1

Higher Power

How we remember our past can shape us, and one of my earliest childhood memories involves destruction. The year was 1969, the year Neil Armstrong landed on the moon, but for me, 1969 was the year Hurricane Camille, one of the worst hurricanes in United States history, took everything from my family.

I was only five years old, and my family lived in Pass Christian, Mississippi, in a small blue house about three miles from the Gulf of Mexico.

When the storm hit, we had to leave our house on Market Street and drive to the Catholic school on 2nd Street, which was even closer to the Gulf. Now, instead of being three miles from the water, we were no more than two blocks up a hill. The logic, I assume, was to get to higher ground for when the water started to rise.

Being so young at the time, I don't remember much about huddling up in the gymnasium at Saint Paul's School, apart from two vivid scenes: (1) a man lying on a table and (2) my dad leading us to higher ground.

When I became an adult, I asked my mom, "What ever happened to that man lying on the table during Hurricane Camille?" She told me that he had died during the storm.

The second, more impactful scene was my dad taking my family through ankle-deep water to the upstairs classrooms. He led me, my mom, and my siblings to higher ground through a corridor with no doors on either side, and although the floor beneath us was built on strong cement blocks, the roof appeared to be held up by aluminum sticks. As the water levels increased, the strong, windy rains plummeted our bodies.

My mom and dad had four children at this time: my brother Errol (eleven), my sister Sharon (eight), me (five), and my sister Juilee (two). I get emotional whenever I think about this scene and all my parents did to keep us safe. Daddy carried me on his back, and my mom carried Juilee, as Errol and Sharon walked. My parents held on to each of us so tight and so close I now knew there was no way we were not all going to make it to safety.

I reflect back on this time to remind myself of how blessed I am. There were many lives lost in Hurricane Camille, yet God saw fit to save ours through the work of my loving parents. To this day, I am so grateful.

Reflection

Reflection is the act of consciously considering the meaning, impact, and feelings surrounding events in your life. When Hurricane Camille hit, I was five years old. I didn't feel scared, and it's obvious now that I really didn't know what was happening. As I reflect on this scene, I'm struck by how close my family was and how we trusted each other to make it through. That is something that has never changed. I learned very early on that storms are meant to bring families and friends closer. I know this may sound like a crazy concept in a world where love appears to be in short supply, but stay with me. The Bible reads in the book of Nahum 1:7, "The Lord is good, a strong hold in the day of trouble; and he knoweth them that trust in him."

I'm not sure if my parents even thought about reading the Bible on that day, but this story reminds me that at the age of five, God had a purpose already laid out for me. Beyond what I've already shared, two other details have convinced me of the higher power working in my life at that time:

1. We were in Saint Paul's Catholic School. *Saint Paul* means "a place of God's refuge."
2. *Camille* is derived from the French, meaning "serving at the altar."

We can make anything mean whatever we want. However, when you begin to recognize how God or your higher power has protected you through no power of your own, it is time to lean in and trust in your higher power!

In order to truly tap into your higher power, you must stop focusing on what your physical eyes see and become one with the spiritual senses deep within you. This means embracing the gut reactions of the limbic system in your brain—the part of your brain that involves personal motivation, emotion, learning, and memory. This area of your brain is not analytical. It's the part of your brain that lets you know in your gut whether something is right or wrong.

What have you always known about your life that you have not stopped and reflected on through your gut feeling? Now is the time to reflect and remember. Tapping into your higher power could very well be the breakthrough you have needed in an area of your personal life. Coupling that with reading the Bible? Man, you will conquer your world!

One more quick story before I leave you with your homework assignment. After Hurricane Camille in 1969, my parents moved us to Chicago, where my Aunt Edriner lived. My dad was still working in Mississippi, so my mom boarded a train with four children by herself and headed to Chi-Town. As an adult, I asked her if she was scared to make that journey and essentially start a new life.

"Scared? Absolutely not! I had four children to take care of."

My mom is the strongest woman I know. I know that is where my strength comes from. I wanted to share this short story because it reminds me of how our higher power protects us from generation to generation.

Lessons Learned

In this chapter, we learned we must find strength in our higher power. To do this, we must:

1. Discover comfort and strength in stories from early childhood memories.
2. Tap into and follow your gut (your limbic system).

Homework Assignment

Where do you get your strength? Not everyone has an Audrey (my mom), but chances are that someone has loved you throughout your entire life.

1. Pause.
2. Close your eyes, and think for five minutes.
3. Look within yourself. God, or your higher power, *always* places someone in your life so that you know you are not alone. Do you see that person? Is there more than one?
4. Write that person(s) name down and hold on to the love and care that's been shared with you.
5. Continue this exercise as many times as necessary to remember as many good memories as you can. Each time, I guarantee you will see the angel(s) God, or your higher power, has placed in your life.

Let me also add this statement: I'm in your life now! And I am telling you that you are strong and valuable, and your higher power is just waiting to be a lamp unto your feet and a light unto your pathway!

I am so grateful for my childhood memories. Not all of them are good, but they made me stronger. Trust the process of life. We are all fearfully and wonderfully made, which means we are valuable beings living a human experience. I encourage you to be a person of value rather than a person of success.

> **Second Tool:** Stop and quiet yourself for five minutes to identify and reflect on good memories from your childhood.

* * *

Mississippi Memories. I was probably two years old in this picture.
That's me in the blue dress and bottle. My sister Sharon front right and my
brother Errol back middle. The other kiddos were my cousins I grew up with.

Age 5

CHAPTER 2

A Reliable, Effective Plan to Serve Others

I n this chapter, I will share a story about a time when I was seven years old to show how I, with my parents' help, established a consistent, reliable, and effective schedule.

If you do not plan out your life, more than likely your life will always appear unreliable, ineffective, and, well, unplanned. If you want to come out of the darkness and find new freedom in your life, you must become intentional. Either you start making your life happen, or life will continue to happen to you. Sorry to be so rough, but anyone who knows me knows that I live by my schedule. The goal isn't to make you obsessive about scheduling, but we do want to create a habit of making plans and then sticking to them.

The first step to creating a consistent schedule is to serve others. I find it easier to become lackluster when serving myself. However, it is how our brain works. If we do something for someone else, we also visualize doing something wonderful for ourselves. However, it is not healthy to give all of yourself to others. There needs to be an allowance for self-care.

Jesus took time to serve and to recuperate. Mark 7:24 reads, "Jesus left that place and went to the vicinity of Tyre. He entered a house and did not want anyone to know it; yet he could not keep his presence secret." Christ used his gifts and talents understanding his purpose and the infinite, impactful possibilities. Although folks kept following Jesus, he did make a point to take time for himself.

Consistent, Streamlined Schedule—A Story

The craft bazaar was about to start, and I felt giddy as I walked out of the kitchen, cake in hand. I scanned the tables in the basement of St. Mary's Church for a place to set down yet another dessert. The church had many bazaars throughout the year, and I would volunteer for them. Even though I was only seven and still relatively new to Toledo, Ohio, I knew my job well. I was a runner, which meant I took treats from the kitchen to the tables. Even as a little black girl surrounded by older white women with grey hair, I never felt out of place. When I think about this memory, I can hear the loud laughter, the huge smiles that made the cheeks on everyone's faces turn red, and the extreme kindness shared by everyone (often in the form of warm bear hugs).

Whenever I came out of the kitchen, an adult always bent down to my height, hugged me, and directed me to the correct table. On this cake run, I passed a lady with quilts and put the cake on the table, before looking back toward the kitchen to see whether I had another assignment.

Although this bazaar is the only recollection I have of serving at this age, the consistent schedule I had at even then still reigns supreme in my mind. It is unimaginable for me to ever think at this point, seven years old, that I knew what I wanted to do with the rest of my life. I knew I wanted to work in schools. I knew that I wanted to work with the elderly. Most importantly, I knew that my family would always support me. It was my mom and dad who made sure I arrived at the bazaar on time to volunteer for each event. It was the training from my parents that helped me develop a lifestyle that is reflective of a consistent, streamlined schedule.

Gifts

While reflecting on this story, I thought deeply about the gifts and talents I used at this age. *Gift* is a word people use all the time, but we often don't take the time to consider the true meaning of our words. One definition of *gift* is "a present or an offering, a donation." The key here is that you are giving and not receiving. And that's the lesson I would like for you to learn right now. While there are certainly physical gifts (presents) we can share with others, there are also ways you can offer yourself and your talents to others. We all have a gift that we can consistently share, and I encourage you to share yours daily. When we share our innate gifts on a consistent, streamlined schedule, the door of opportunity opens. As written in Proverbs 18:16, "A man's gift makes room for him and brings him before great men."

If we think of our gifts as offerings or donations, it becomes obvious that our gifts are not for us to keep. Your gifts are meant to be donations for the good of the world. Donate to your community. Donate your gift so it can be used to make someone else happy and to encourage others. Without a doubt, consider a consistent, streamlined schedule that will allow you to donate your gifts to others.

Talent, Purpose, and Possibility

Thinking of the word *gift* in this way invites us to explore the words *talent*, *purpose*, and *possibility*. A talent is a natural skill. Purpose is when you do something with determination and intention in mind. And possibility is the likelihood something will occur.

Your talent, purpose, and possibilities can be found as you reflect on your childhood and consider how you served others and yourself.

I started this chapter sharing with you how I served at my church as a very young child. I used my natural skills and my talents to make a difference in the lives of others. Therefore, the possibility (i.e., the likelihood) of serving others occurring over and over in my life was extremely high. Yet, I vaguely remember ever learning to really serve myself.

Talent In More Detail

The following parable describes how several servants received talents.

The Parable of the Talent

Taken from Max Lucado, *Cure for the Common Life.*

Matthew 25:14–15

> *For the Kingdom of Heaven is like a man traveling to a far country who called his own servants and delivered his Goods to them and to one he gave five talents to another two talents and to another one talent to each according to his own ability and immediately he went on a journey.*

Before "talent" meant skill, it meant money. It represented the largest unit of accounting in the Greek currency 10,000 denarii. According to the parable of the workers, a denarius representing a day's fair wages (Matthew 20:22). Multiply your daily wage by 10,000 and you discover the value of a talent. If you earn $30,000 a year and you annually work 260 days, you make about $115 a day. A talent in your case is valued at 10,000 times $115 or $1,150,000.

Place this in perspective. Suppose a person earns $30,000 a year for forty years. Her lifetime earnings are $1,200,000 only $50,000 more than a talent. One talent, then, equals a lifetime of earnings. This is a lot of money and a key point in this parable. Your god-given design and uniqueness have high market value in heaven. God didn't entrust you with a $2 talent or a $5 skill. Consider yourself a million-dollar investment—in many cases, a multimillion-dollar enterprise.

The point of detailing the talent from Max Lucado's book is that if you have one or more talents, you are financially rich. Yes, serve others with your talents, but also serve yourself. Learn to set boundaries so you can manifest your dreams and visions.

Purpose In More Detail

Have you ever thought about your purpose? Even if you have, let's talk about individual purpose as I describe it here. First of all, we are created beings, and that means our spiritual purpose is to worship and glorify God, our Creator. The Bible teaches in *I Corinthians 10:31, "Whether therefore ye eat, or drink, or whatsoever ye do, do all to the glory of God."*

As you consider your purpose, know that you can find it in the dreams and visions you see over and over in your head. Your purpose is how you showed up as a youth to class and sporting events. Your purpose is how you showed up with your friends. Your purpose is to approach the world in a godly way, using your talents to be a light unto the world, for the glory of God.

What gifts or talents did you bring to the table? Were you the leader or were you a team member? How you showed up then is more than likely how you are showing up now— good or bad, leader or follower. If you are reading this book and are not following your dreams and visions, then I can guarantee your life shifted away from your purpose and what God wants for you. Instead of you navigating life by following your purpose (your dreams and visions), chances are you brushed off your dreams and visions. You may be handling this reality with class and a smile, but behind closed doors, there may be moments when you are sad and frustrated. On the other hand, you may be handling your shifted life like a grumpy bull in a china shop. Either way, it is time to stop! Together, we are going to shift you back to following your purpose.

Has anyone ever told you that you can have more than one purpose? Well, it's true. You have more than one dream and vision, right? Therefore, you can have more than one purpose. As I mentioned earlier, set boundaries to manifest your dreams and visions. You can do that by creating effective, consistent schedules.

For years, I showed up as an adult as I did as a youth— consistently ready to serve others and *not* myself. I've since learned to take care of myself, consistently and on a schedule. Realizing the importance of caring for myself was the breakthrough I needed to begin shifting my own life toward my purpose. I pray that as you go through each chapter, you will receive your breakthrough too, as you intentionally and consistently streamline your schedule for personal inner growth.

Lessons Learned

In this chapter, we learned:
1. Consistency and scheduling can begin at an early age.
2. We can determine what our innate gifts and talents are by serving others.
3. Your purpose can be directly connected to your dreams and visions.
4. Your purpose can be directly connected to how you showed up in life as a youth.

Homework Assignment

Develop a habit of creating a consistent, streamlined schedule.

In his book *The Power of Habit*, Charles Duhigg explains how one small shift in perception can develop a "keystone habit." This keystone habit, or small shift, will help you develop and create a consistent, streamlined schedule.
1. To discover your purpose, begin by writing your gifts.
   a. Not sure of your gifts? See the table of adjectives in the endnotes.
   b. Identify your purpose based on the adjectives you described. For example, if you are consistent, calm, and fair, being a good listener and encourager might be your gift.
   c. Embody the adjectives you used to describe yourself in your daily interactions. Begin living out your purpose.
2. Every night or morning, write down what you have to accomplish that day, week, month, or year.
3. Every night or morning, write down how you can serve both yourself and others with your gifts and talents.
4. Maintain a journal of your dreams and visions.

Third Tool: Purchase a calendar with pages to create a to-do list, and use it.

* * *

CHAPTER 3

Motivate, Pray, and Learn the OK's

Throughout this book, I will continue to share stories from my life and draw from them insights that can help you transform your own life. You may have never examined your life in this way, but each story in your own life truly matters. Not only does it matter to you, but it matters to those to whom God has assigned you. In this chapter, I am going to share three stories about experiences I had when I was nine and ten. The stories I share were formative for me, and because of their significance, you will see their ripple effects as you continue into other chapters. This should not come as a surprise. We all have stories that repeat over and over in our minds because they are entangled with our emotions. Your emotions represent three areas: your circumstance, your mood, and your relationship with others. I think these stories are funny, and I hope you enjoy them.

The Black Dress

At ten years old, I realized my mom owned a black negligee. It was a long, beautiful thing with spaghetti straps and a V-neck collar. Whenever there was a major dinner—usually for Christmas, Thanksgiving, or Easter—I would dress up in my mom's black negligee, running upstairs to take off my clothes and slip it on, over the shirt I wore underneath. I'd fix my hair in a dressy style, walk down the steps, and go into the dining room. Every time, my family would look at me and laugh. "You are crazy!" they'd say. "Why do you have on that black dress?" But nothing they said ever bothered me. I felt pretty. I felt important. I felt smart. I didn't have time to care what anyone said about me.

That is when I knew I could motivate myself. After that first dinner, I made sure I did not need anyone to motivate me. I did not need anyone to show me that I belonged or that I mattered. I knew it for myself, and that black dress meant everything to me.

I looked good in my mother's long, black, spaghetti-string, down-to-the-ankles negligee!

Why do I tell this story? I hope to remind you of a time when you were so fierce and sure of yourself that you were able to walk in a room full of hecklers with your own (probably metaphorical) long, black dress. But if you have never experienced the superpower of not caring what people think, use my story. Walk in my fearlessness to get started on a new journey where you can focus on your future and not worry about what people think. Walk daily with a smile on your face, knowing in your heart you have power that comes from within.

Prayer Works

The next story is not so much related to me but is about what happened to my baby sister when I was ten.

My sister had just been born and brought home. My parents had gone out to dinner, and my brother and I sat on the couch with my grandmother Alverine, who was holding my baby sister. All of a sudden, my grandmother screamed as loud as a person riding a roller coaster. My baby sister had started shaking as if she was being electrocuted. And, somehow the whites of her eyes began to change color! She was shaking and the shaking did not stop, and everyone began to panic.

I do not remember exactly who called my parents, but they came home immediately. By this point, everyone was still panicking—but not me. I ran up the first flight of steps, turned, and ran up the second flight of steps. Once I reached the top, I headed straight to my bedroom and grabbed my rosary, the beads Catholics use to say their prayers. I tore down both flights of steps and began to walk around the living room, praying the rosary.

On the rosary, there are ten beads where you say the Hail Mary prayer, and when you reach the biggest bead or the bead that separates the ten beads, you say the Lord's Prayer. I went through each prayer, repeating them over and over. While I prayed, my brother paced angrily until he punched his hand through the window of the front door. I stopped only for a moment, then went back to praying. As I prayed for the health and the recovery of my baby sister, our lives shifted.

I am happy to write that my baby sister is alive and well. Just days old, she almost died from a virus that caused a fever so high it sent her into convulsions. Today, she is an educator in the urban schools of Toledo, Ohio and recently obtained her EdD in leadership.

I believe prayer saved my sister, and I still believe that prayer changes lives. Prayer creates new meaning for the situations in our lives. It's our belief in God, and it's our prayer lives that make a difference in the lives of others.

Fourth Grade

This last story is one I'm not proud of. But as you journey with me through my life, I am going to have to show you both my good side and my bad side.

I often do not use the word *bad* when it comes to describing children, but it certainly describes the kind of child I was. There is honestly no other way to describe my behavior at the time of this story. Let me prove it.

By the time I entered Mrs. O'Johnson's fourth-grade class, I did not find myself very pretty. Because I was darker, my sisters would tease me and call me Spooky John. And since my hair was extremely coarse, they would call me Pick-a-Ninny. Over time, the way I started to view myself was not very kind. Add on to that I was at a new school (our family had just moved across town) and I did not have friends, and it's unsurprising that I was on the verge of an emotional disaster.

I always knew that as long as I served and helped others, I would receive positive affirmation and be noticed by those in authority. What I didn't know was that although outside affirmation is great, inner belief in one's self is needed to bring the most joy and stability in life.

At this time, I was working with my dad at ServiceMaster as a janitor. He would wake me up on Saturday and Sunday mornings to go clean school buildings and banks with him. I became a really good cleaner, and my dad loved when I helped him. In the classroom, I helped clean all the time. While I'd like to say I only did this because I knew I could make a difference, the truth of the matter is I just wanted to be liked. I wanted to be liked by the teacher, and I wanted to be liked by the kids. I knew I was smart and athletic, but because of my insecurities, I just couldn't be as outgoing as I wanted to be. The best I could do was volunteer, smile, and work hard.

Although I worked hard in fourth grade to avoid making any waves, I still was teased, especially by one individual. Everyone loved her, but I really could not understand why. She was so crude, talked about everyone, and called people names. Still, everyone still liked her.

Since I was a class volunteer and leader, I was able to be in the classroom by myself. On this particular day, while the kids were eating lunch, I walked down the long hallway past the cafeteria and went into the classroom to put books from the bookshelf on all the desks. As I came to Mean Girl's desk, I felt the overwhelming urge to cover the inside of it with glue. I opened the desk, feeling so angry and frustrated at all the things she'd said about me, and slathered glue over everything inside—all over her books, her papers, her pencils. Everything. As I closed the desk and put the glue back in my own desk, my heart raced when I heard the other students coming back to the classroom.

Once the class resumed Mrs. O'Johnson asked everyone to open their desks and pull out a paper and pencil to write. I thought I would die and puke on myself. I never turned my head to see the girl's expression, but I can still hear her screeching as she saw the damaged contents of her desk. That day, I made the decision that I never wanted to be hurtful or harm anyone ever again. Although the word *bully* was not used at this time, I knew I would never retaliate or try to get back at someone just because they were unkind.

I never looked up at Mrs. O'Johnson. She knew that I did it—I was the only one who had access to the classroom—but the incident was not reported, and I did not get in trouble. Even still, the hurt and the memory of doing something so hateful sticks with me.

Reflection

I now understand that no matter how young you are and no matter how crude anyone is to you, it is important to make sure you do not internalize the situation. Someone else's bad behavior toward you is rarely ever about you.

Here's another shocking realization: life is so weird. When you are a child, you just want to be liked and just want to get along. With great disappointment, I have to admit that I brought these characteristics into my adult life.

I am so grateful to finally be writing this book because I can continue my growth as a person, both as a human and a spiritual being. I also know what it takes to become the best version of myself by reflecting on my experiences. More importantly, I can help others become the best version of themselves.

I have come to the understanding that not all of us are going to get along. I encourage you to focus on the following three items:

1. Always believe in God and the scripture that says that you have been fearfully and wonderfully created.
2. Know that even when your self-esteem is low and you do not have any friends, *loneliness* and *being alone* are two different things. Just because you are alone does not mean you are lonely. (I learned this from my son, Alan.) You can always have a friend, and you can always make a connection with someone. You just have to find your tribe. You just have to find your circle. And guess what? If you never find a tribe or circle, you can still believe in God and the truth the Bible tells you: "He said, I will never leave you nor forsake you." That will be your start. If you need ideas about where to make connections, consider going to church or volunteering at a library, senior center, nursing home, or school within your community.
3. Live by faith. The strength and power God will provide every single day. Soon enough you'll declare, "Even if I'm alone, I'm not lonely."

Once you are comfortable in your own skin, confidently flaunting your long, black dress, your life and your relationships will shift toward the better. To help you get to that point, always remember the three OKs:

1. It's OK when people are being mean to you; it really is.
2. It's OK when people don't like you; it really is.
3. It's OK when you don't fit in; it really is.

The takeaway from the three OKs:

1. You learn not to be mean to yourself.
2. You learn to love yourself.
3. You learn to be by yourself.

Lessons Learned

1. Motivate yourself daily with encouraging words. Put on clothes that make you feel good. Enjoy quiet time with yourself.
2. Prayer is essential to your emotional stability. As written in 1 Thessalonians 5:16–17, "Rejoice always, pray without ceasing, give thanks in all circumstances; for this is the will of God in Christ Jesus for you."
3. Human life is OK because you can thrive spiritually with God.

Homework Assignment

For the next thirty days write a prayer, motivating yourself from the inside out.

For example: Lord, today I am encouraged that you are directing my thoughts and my emotions. I thank you and I praise you for being with me every moment of my life. In Jesus's name, amen

Fourth Tool: Pause on purpose.
Find a quiet space and complete your homework.

* * *

A Prophetic Word I heard from God to share with you

I truly want you to know how much I love you! I understand that human life can be hard. That is why I sent my Son to show you how to live a simple life. Focus on me. Do not become overwhelmed with the problems of this world nor the people in it. Focus on building your spiritual being, and you will find a peace that passes all understanding. Thus says the Lord.

Family—the living room

CHAPTER 4

Your Life Story Matters

By high school, I was popular. I made the cheerleading team and was named captain for the squads I was on. I was class president my sophomore, junior and senior years. I was on the junior and senior homecoming courts, and I was made homecoming queen my senior year. Also in my senior year, I was named treasurer of the student government and started as editor-in-chief of our yearbook, the *Scottonian*. But while I was having the time of my life, I was also having the worst time of my life. See, I had secrets, and lots of them. I was part of many scandals and told so many lies throughout high school. Worst of all, I would never finish out my senior year.

I prayed a long time before I really searched my soul to decide which stories I would share—the ones that would do the most to help others become strong, solid soldiers in life. The following stories describe heartache and healing, hatred and love, hurt and forgiveness. I pray no one ever has to experience the hurt and pain that I both caused and endured.

Life with God

Before I explain more about my high school experience, a little more background is needed. I attended Catholic school most of elementary school, and I remember clearly sitting in the classroom on the second floor of Cathedral School, located two blocks from my home on Collingwood Street.

I loved religion class and being focused on the Bible and all its teachings. (This class, of course, supplemented the sermons of the priest every Monday morning at Mass). Every day at 9:00 a.m., we would have religion class, and I can still sense the calm and peace that would come over me as the teacher taught lessons on Jesus and his love for us.

I was ten years old and in fifth grade when I made the decision to become a nun. I practiced being a nun on special occasions during dinner time with my family. Yes, that's why I wore my mom's long, black dress. I had no idea I was wearing lingerie, much less the irony of leading grace at the dinner table while wearing lingerie. I just knew serving people and the Lord was the calling on my life.

As I entered sixth grade at Cathedral Catholic School, there was another school, Old West End Junior High School, being built on the opposite end of our neighborhood. My parents were educators in inner city Toledo, my mom a principal at an elementary school in our neighborhood and my dad a math teacher at Scott High School. Since the new school was being built, it would be a new experience to everyone in the neighborhood, my parents asked me if I wanted to attend public schools. That summer after sixth grade, I entered the public school system, and that decision shifted me toward the life I now know, for better and for worse.

The Shift from Parochial to Public Schools

I finished my last year at Cathedral Catholic School feeling smart, full of God, and sure that I was going to be a nun one day. Because of the books that I was reading throughout the summer, I entered Old West End Junior High School with confidence and a plan to succeed.

At twelve years old, I was a leader at Old West End in many ways. A great student and a great athlete, I was chosen to be a part of the student body government. In no time at all, I became engrossed in the activities of public school, which were so different from the activities of Catholic school. My life shifted almost overnight. I no longer thought about God. I no longer thought about religion. I even started thinking about boys!

The students were also different in the sense that they were confident of who they were in the world. There was also an atmosphere that seemed free and fun in comparison. If only I'd known the old cliché, "what's fun ain't always free."

Short Lesson

If you are in a group where even one person is making bad decisions, learn from their mistakes. This is advice I never took for myself.

When you come into a world with a different atmosphere than you're used to, you need to show up differently. You are never too young (or old) to learn how to show up ready to work hard and make good decisions everyday. Even adults can change their habits and start making good decisions.

There is a passage in the Bible that reads, "Finally, brethren, whatsoever things are true, whatsoever things are honest, whatsoever things are just, whatsoever things are pure, whatsoever things are lovely, whatsoever things are of good report; if there be any virtue, and if there be any praise, think on these things" (Philippians 4:8).

I prayed and read the Word of God from a little girl through age eleven. I did not read and pray as much between the ages of twelve and eighteen. Looking back at the transition away from parochial school, I did not know what I did not know. Today I encourage you to be aware of the shifting in your life. Feel it. Know it. When the shifting is good, take advantage of it. The window of opportunity to embrace that change in your life may only stay open for a short time. When you feel the shifting is bad, take note and make the necessary changes to avoid more of it. I was not aware of the shift in my young life. I did not see or feel it coming. Yet when the shift came, I followed it, and my life went down what I would like to call Bad-Shift Avenue.

Story Time

Here are two stories that show how I allowed my life to shift instead of me shifting my life.

The Shift from Parochial to Public Schools, Part Two

At Old West End Junior High School, I discovered boys. Different boys. Boys that looked like me. (I don't remember ever seeing black boys at Cathedral Catholic School.) In this new world, there were boys, and I noticed them.

The energy and the mindset at Old West End Junior High School were not like the ones at Cathedral Catholic School. Instead of wearing uniforms, we wore cute, colorful dresses and Gloria Vanderbilt blue jeans. All around, people made an effort to appear stylish. Before, I didn't want my mom to comb my hair, and I never learned to fix it up myself. Once I got to public school, I needed her (desperately) to style my hair. The kids would always compare who wore the best outfit. The girls would talk about which guy was the best looking. I do not remember there being much talk about the classes we attended.

Because of all these new captivating ideas—fashion, style, hair, and yes, boys—I remember how quickly I began rethinking my career as a nun. Nuns had to wear habits, long, black robes that hang down to their ankles, and a black head dressing with a white band on the front. I know you all know, but this does not scream "high fashion."

As a nun, I would have had to read the Bible, teach about the Bible, or teach school all day long. But I wanted my own life. I wanted to have a boyfriend. Everyone else had one, and I should have one too, I thought, even if my mom and dad said no.

Then I found out at twelve years old that nuns took a vow to not have sex. There I was, in a public school with a different group of kids that were talking about sex and had boyfriends, yet I came from a parochial school and didn't know anything about any of that! My life had shifted, and I allowed it to continue shifting instead of making a change.

Even though I had a lot to learn about life in a public school, I gained many friends. We were all on the same page about our education and earned stellar grades. Most of my friends had both parents at home at that time, but even though we all came from decent families, we still were challenging kids. That didn't improve when I got a boyfriend.

I had one boyfriend in seventh and eighth grade. He did not attend Old West End, but his brother did, and through him we met. After that, I had a boyfriend, y'all. I had a boyfriend! He was two years older than me and was a freshman in high school. Thus began my thing for older guys (just kidding).

Although I called him my boyfriend, my dad really did not consider him as such. He would come around the house, and we talked and laughed and actually kissed a couple times. He was a really, nice guy, and he never pressured me to do anything I wasn't comfortable with. Right before starting my freshman year in high school, though, I made the decision to break up with him. I wanted to see the kind of boys I'd find in high school.

The Brick Conversation

During the summer of 1978, Tonya Marie Patterson, a.k.a. Queen T and now my friend of forty years, sat with me on the bricks outside my parent's brown, four-bedroom home.

"Tonya, I'm going to find my boyfriend right when I get to Scott High School," I said enthusiastically.

"Michelle, what?" Tonya exclaimed.

Tonya and I had been thick as thieves for the past two years since I entered Old West End Junior High School. We were like the comedians Laurel and Hardy. I was always creating ideas, and Tonya always poked holes in them.

"I'm telling you," I continued, "there are some really cute boys at Scott High School. I have already looked through the yearbook three times."

"What?!" Tonya exclaimed again.

"I'll go get the yearbook!" I barreled through the back door as fast as a horse in the Kentucky Derby, up two flights of steps to my oldest sister's room, grabbed her 1978 Scott High School yearbook, and then made my way back outside. On that beautiful June day, I returned to see my Tonya, my Hardy, patiently waiting on the bricks to listen to every idea I had cooped up in my head.

We opened the yearbook, and I pointed to a sophomore I'd had my eye on. His name was Kelvin Spears.

"That's going to be my boyfriend," fourteen-year-old me told her.

No matter what happened, I was going to make sure that young man in that yearbook was going to be my boyfriend when I entered high school.

Lessons Learned

Become aware of the small shifts in your life, or they could potentially cause major harm in the future.

Homework Assignment:

1. Write down the small events that occurred in your life that have caused your life to shift.
2. Write down how those shifts affected you. If any of the effects were negative, resolve them as best you can, and ask for help when needed.
3. Write down five events you would like to occur in your life. Writing your thoughts down is the first step in making them happen. Then write down three steps you will take to start preparing for the events, starting with steps you can take today.

Fifth Tool: Purchase a journal—a big one! You can make your own with a spiral notebook. Use it as a space to write down your homework assignments for this chapter.

* * *

The Brick Conversation

Tonya "Queen-T" Patterson
Gail and Oprah—Thelma and Louise

Junior Class Officers

1981-1982 HOMECOMING QUEEN

MICHELLE JEFFRIES

Michelle Jeffries

Senior

Picture from the Scottonian Year Book

Freshman

Freshman

Freshman

Junior

Senior

CHAPTER 5

My Parents Knew

It was the first day of high school, and I wanted to dress to impress. I was not sure how high school kids dressed, and I didn't have my sister Sharon to help me since she had graduated a year earlier than expected. Still, I was excited because I knew I would soon have the boyfriend of my dreams. After all, I had hand-picked him out of hundreds!

The morning was going by fast when I ran into a young man who was also a freshman. We apologized for running into each other and ran through the usual first-day-of-school greetings, when I realized I had a potential source of information.

"Hey, I'm looking for a specific guy. I saw his picture in last year's yearbook and really would love to meet him."

"Who is the guy?" he asked.

"His name is Kelvin." His freshman face lit up. "I know him!"

"You do?!?"

"Yeah, I'll take you to him."

I could not believe this was happening. I was going to meet the guy in the yearbook picture, the guy Tonya and I talked about all summer. I was about to meet him face to face.

I could hardly contain my excitement. We literally took off running down the hallway to the middle steps of Scott High School. The middle steps of the school were significant, I quickly found out, because if you had a locker on the second floor in the middle hallway, you were considered popular. Well, guess where my dream boyfriend's locker was located? In the middle of the second floor. Oh my! He was cute *and* popular!

My excitement was building, I didn't even notice how quickly we ran up the first flight of steps from the first floor. Just one more turn and a few steps away from where the popular kids had their lockers, I started getting nervous. As we rounded the corner, I looked up and I saw my boyfriend. My heart was in the clouds. I could not believe how handsome, how fine this brother was!

Five foot eight, he had a deep chocolate brown complexion, huge afro, and the biggest, whitest smile with the prettiest teeth that you could ever imagine! I was so enamored with him I completely ignored the hint of acne on his cheeks. That did not matter. He was so fine, and I knew that he was mine! Such a corny statement for me to make, but it was so true for me at that time.

Now standing right in front of him, all shyness, insecurity and self-doubt were gone.

My new friend got my new boyfriend's attention. "Hey, Kelvin. This is—"

"Hi, my name is Michelle," I interrupted. "How are you?"

"Good," he replied with a shiny, white half-smile. "How are you?"

"I'm just excellent! Can we meet and talk later?" I asked, taking notice of all his friends around him. I didn't care that they were watching us. I just wanted the chance to get to know him one on one.

"Sure."

Later that day, before school was out, Kelvin found me in one of my classes, and we exchanged phone numbers. He called me that same night, and I remember talking to him until we both fell asleep.

Simply by dreaming him up, I got the boyfriend I'd always hoped I'd get!

The romance was amazing. He would meet me in the morning when I got to school, take my books, and walk me to class. At each class break, he would meet me and walk me to my next class. I thought he was the sweetest person ever. I even started attending church with him on Sunday mornings since his father was a pastor.

Then, it happened. Sex. It didn't take long for us to take that step. I remember my mother asking, "Shelly, are you having sex?" Of course, I immediately told her no, thus beginning my lying streak, first with my parents, then with other family members and friends.

Reflection

I was fourteen years old, having sex, and telling my new dream boyfriend, "I love you." Fourteen? I still shake my head looking back and wonder what I was thinking. Why did I not know how wrong this picture looked? My parents knew. My parents knew all too well. They did everything to remind me.

I can still hear my dad's voice: "Have fun in school, Michelle. Do not have a boyfriend in school. It makes things too emotional. Wait until you are older to have a boyfriend. Focus on your studies."

As I reflect back on the conversations I had with my parents, I remember how I thought of their warnings. It all sounded like the teacher in the Charlie Brown cartoon was speaking: "Wah waaah, wah, wah." What did they know?

A lot, actually. Moreover, I should have listened. By this time, Kelvin's and my emotional connection had grown, but what we thought was love was just emotional chaos. Humans have nine basic emotions: anger, fear, love, joy, surprise, sadness, disgust, shame, and pride. Kelvin and I were too young to understand how to navigate any of them. There was no conscious direction, especially when it came to the emotions triggered by sex. Once the sex started, the worst of the emotions prevailed. We started dating on the first school day in September, 1978, and were fighting verbally daily by basketball season in December. Soon enough, we'd fight physically and consistently, even up until the day he died.

Lessons Learned

Listen to parents, teachers, and guardians who provide wise, mature counsel.

Homework Assignment

Integrate the wise, mature counsel you receive from parents, teachers, or guardians.

Sixth Tool: Purchase and read Brene Brown's book *Raising Strong*.

* * *

CHAPTER 6

Shifting More

S enior year. I was captain of the cheerleading squad and won the election for class president against Steve White, one of my best friends, even today. He and I were ecstatic at the situation, because that meant he would also serve as class vice president. We were (and still are) close, and I needed him to keep all my secrets, along with a few other homies: my BFF Tonya, my sister Juilee, and my cousin Terrie.

By the time I was seventeen, Kelvin and I had broken up too many times to count. We fought in public so many times that everyone knew how volatile our relationship was. My homies tried their best to keep the peace, a.k.a. keeping us apart. That just never worked.

I will not go through each story of abuse and fight in detail, but a few that were extremely violent, and at this point in my life, I'm sad to realize how stupid they were. We had no idea how much we were hurting ourselves or those around us.

Although these stories actually occurred, hear me clearly: both of us were at fault. Neither of us were blameless, yet I believe Kelvin and I loved each other deeply in the best way we knew how.

No Details, Just Results

One night in front of my cousin Terrie's house, Kelvin hit me so hard in the mouth it busted my chin and loosened my front bottom tooth. But I dished it out too. Once I busted Kelvin's back window of his car after I caught him cheating with another girl. Needless to say, my mom and dad whipped me so much that I had a black and blue bruise on my right thigh by the time I left their bedroom. It took over a week for the bruise just to stop hurting, and then another week for the bruise to finally start fading.

Even after these incidents we stayed together and we kept cussing and fussing at each other in front of our friends. Our arguments had become the norm for everyone. But there was nothing normal about that kind of behavior. If you have a friend that is violently fighting at any age, get them help.

This all happened during the fall of my senior year, and my parents once again banned Kelvin from coming over to the house. I did my best to hide most of the fights from them, but whenever they found out, my relationship with Kelvin went on hiatus, as far as my parents knew. Kelvin and I—we always found a way to see each other.

Homecoming, 1981

It was homecoming season, and I was the homecoming queen. But even though this was a shining moment of my high school career, it was tarnished by the fact that Kelvin had been banned from my life yet again, leaving me dateless.

I can hear my mother's warning, "If you guys do not stop fighting, someone's name is going to end up in the paper."

I so wish that I listened to her words, but they were drowned out by my protests.

The Saturday after being announced as homecoming queen, I put on my dress and crown, and went down to the living room to get my picture taken, alone and without a date. I went to the homecoming dance by myself, or so my parents thought. When I reached the school parking lot, Kelvin was waiting for me, just as we'd planned. We walked in as if we came to the homecoming dance together.

Even after our recent fights, we had so much fun together that night. After the homecoming dance, we did what we'd done throughout the summer and the beginning of the school year: we snuck away to be together. That Saturday night, I conceived and became pregnant with our only daughter.

Early Graduation

I fought with other people besides Kelvin at school, and my parents were sick of it. I'd made plenty of enemies, and eventually some of that caught up with me. Over homecoming weekend, students who did not like me called our house to tell me how much they hated me becoming homecoming queen. "You were not the people's choice!" they'd say. Some would just tie up the line, calling and hanging up over and over. Others would flat out call me a bitch and tell me that they planned to beat me up at school on Monday. My parents, of course, had to deal with all this drama, and if they weren't already fed up enough those phone calls were the last straw.

The Monday after homecoming, my dad came to school, walked into my classroom, and told the teacher he needed to take me to the office. We walked there in a silence only broken by my father asking the office clerk to check my grades. "I want to make sure she has enough credits to graduate," he said.

Graduate? Why was he so worried about that? I had an entire school year to complete.

I graduated in October of 1981. I never finished my entire Senior year. I never got to experience being homecoming queen for an entire year. I never got to live out my role as senior class president. And I never walked across a stage to receive my high school diploma. When my friends were throwing up their caps, I was nine months pregnant.

Kelvin at graduation... that's
me to the right black dress

You had to guess who this
was in our year book

Homecoming 1981

Terrie Landry Cook
My cousin by blood, sister through love
and friends by choice

CHAPTER 7

Pregnant Beginnings

Audrei (pronounced, "Audrey") was born June 19, 1982. Like many women who have children at a very young age, I dug deep and found the internal motherly instinct I needed to get through this part of my life. But let's face it—getting pregnant as a teenage girl is a mistake. Most teenagers are still learning to take care of themselves. What happens when you add a child into the mix? I may not have had the mindset to understand how to deal with the mistake I made, but like other young mothers, I learned how to handle mistakes with the love that people showed me.

Kelvin and his family were supportive throughout my entire pregnancy, but that didn't keep the future father of my child and I from fighting during my pregnancy. I share this because I want you to know how emotionally vulnerable and insecure I was during my pregnancy. I sincerely hope that no one has to go through the kind of emotional trauma I suffered through as a pregnant teen. Fighting anyone during your pregnancy (or any other time) is never worth the toll it takes on you. As a pregnant mother, your role is to take care of both yourself and your child. At seventeen, I could hardly take care of myself. I did not see myself as significant or loved, just as a girl who had made so many mistakes.

My mom told me once, "Shelly, you have lived the life of two grown women."

Two grown women.

Today, I understand what my mom was saying. A teenage girl should never be in an adult relationship. No teenage boy either! Unfortunately, with social media and such easy access to adult content, it is very difficult to keep track of what our children are watching. Please learn from my mistakes and take the extra effort to protect your kids. I have grandchildren now, and I pray the lessons I've learned have taught me enough to ensure they do not lose their way as I did.

Six Months Pregnant: The Beginning

After my dad made me graduate in October of 1981, he and my mom thought it would be best for me to move to Pass Christian, Mississippi, where I was born, and live with my dad's parents, Grandma Pam and Grandpa Bowly. I, of course, hated the idea and told my parents I hated them for sending me. I lived in Mississippi for thirty horrible days. Even though my grandparents were absolutely wonderful people, I just wanted to be in Toledo, sneaking around with Kelvin. Meanwhile, my parents, who didn't even know I was pregnant yet, were doing everything they could to protect me and Kelvin. We just did not see it.

After calling my parents almost every day, screaming and crying to come home, they allowed me to return if I agreed to attend college and stay away from Kelvin. In a heartbeat, I accepted. I was seventeen and just wanted to come home. I would have promised to eat dirt if I had to. With my mind not on school, I flunked out of college almost right away, just as my mother had predicted. And I immediately started sneaking around to see Kelvin.

It was February 28, 1982—my dad's birthday. I walked in my parent's bedroom with a pamphlet and set it in the middle of their bed. My mom put down the book she was reading, picked up the pamphlet and quickly tossed it to my dad, clearly not happy.

"What is this?" Daddy asked.

"She's pregnant."

I thought, Michelle, you are a horrible person. How could you tell your dad you were pregnant on his birthday? But I had kept that secret from them for a long time, and I had to tell them.

My father turned, looked at me, steam coming out of both ears, and his body shot to the moon and back.

"What is wrong with you?" he screamed.

That was all it took. I immediately dashed out of the room, down the stairs, and out the front door. By the time I reached the street corner, I heard my mother calling from a window.

"Shelly! Shelly, come back!"

I just kept running, her voice fading until I could hear her no more. I did not stop running until I reached my uncle Earl's house, about a mile from my home. I was a cross-country runner, so a mile was not a long distance for me at all. My uncle was not at home, but my aunt Betty, his wife, opened the door.

"Michelle?" she asked. "Girl, get in here. What are you doing?"

Aunt Betty was my protector to a fault, back in the day. "I was crying uncontrollably, and Aunt Betty took me in the kitchen to calm me down, as she'd done so many times before. Sadly, it would not be the last. My cousin Terrie sat right there with me. She has always been right there with me.

My parents, of course, knew where to find me. They picked me up that night and took me home. My mother's words were so calming.

"Shelly, get some rest. We will figure this out in the morning."

The next morning, my parents went to work. At this point in her career, my mom was a junior high counselor, and my dad now worked with at-risk youth as an occupational work educator. This meant he taught classes half the day and found the students jobs the second half of the day. (I am sure he became an expert in his field, in part, by having me as his daughter.)

My mom left instructions in the kitchen for me to call the doctor's office, and she then made several follow-up calls throughout the day to check on me and the status of the calls.

March 1982

Before telling my parents I was pregnant, I was running three miles five days a week at the city park. I was having regular menstrual cycles, so I never thought I was pregnant. Once I missed two cycles, I became scared. But given that there were not many signs that I was pregnant—my stomach was flat and everything!—I figured I was not that far along when my parents took me to the doctor. To our surprise, the doctor came out and told me and my parents that I was six months pregnant.

We were all shocked. My parents thanked the doctor and listened to his instructions about beginning prenatal care. As we walked out of the office, I looked down at my stomach and watched it grow before my eyes. We drove home in silence.

When a woman tells you she had no idea she was pregnant, believe her. I hadn't a clue. But God did.

> *"'For my thoughts are not your thoughts, neither are your ways my ways,' declares the Lord. 'As the heavens are higher than the Earth, so are my ways higher than your ways and my thoughts than your thoughts.'" Isaiah 55:8–9*

The Call

I called Kelvin on the phone again. No answer. At this point Kelvin had stopped attending college and was sharing an apartment with his brother. Since finding out I was pregnant, my parents had allowed me to start seeing him again and allowed him to come to the house.

I kept calling and calling.

I had a gut feeling he was at the apartment, so at six months pregnant (showing big time) and with literally no money, I called a cab. What was I thinking?

The cab picked me up and drove me to where Kelvin was living. I got out and had no idea how I was going to get back home. Looking back as I write this story, I can feel how unstable I was. I was out of my conscious mind which made prey to my emotions. I walked slowly from the dark corner to the apartment building. I was cold, scared, nervous, and angry about what I was going to find. Even with those emotions driving me, I walked up and knocked on the door.

Bam! Bam! Bam!

I knocked as hard as I could and then peeked through the peephole. I knocked again. Peering through the peephole again, I could see Kelvin walking toward the door. His shirt was off, and I heard him zip his pants as he opened the door.

A girl ran from his bedroom to the bathroom. Pumped full of pregnancy hormones, I went ballistic. I pushed Kelvin to the side and took off running toward the bathroom. I wanted to know who the girl was.

A note to all pregnant women: If the guy wants to mess around and doesn't want you during the pregnancy, leave him. It doesn't get better. It will only get worse. I encourage you to decide sooner rather than later to just move on.

When I reached the bathroom, I kicked the door down and I reached out to grab and punch the girl. Instead of Kelvin protecting me, he pulled me back. The girl was only wearing underwear and a bra, the rest of her clothes and her high-heel shoes in her arms.

I was dizzy from Kelvin grabbing me, and I could hear him yelling to the other girl, "Run, get out of here!"

Before the girl ran out, she hit me on the back side of my head with the heel of her shoe.

As Kelvin held me immobile, I screamed, "She's hitting me! She's hitting me in my head!"

Since then, I've had dizzy spells and bad headaches for over thirty years. In April, 2013, I lost the hearing in my left ear. This isn't a professional diagnosis, but I'm certain it all comes back to that hit in the head.

As if this story isn't clear enough, remember that a relationship lacks love when chaos is involved! It is not worth jeopardizing your health or the life of your child. Toxic relationships bring pain—physical, mental, and emotional. The last two are the real danger because they take so much longer to remove from your life. I was living a life of hell by staying stuck in the world Kelvin and I created.

After the girl hit me in the head with her stiletto heel, Kelvin pulled me back again and yelled at the girl to run. She took off, running out of the apartment. After she left, Kelvin and I began to yell at each other. He reached out and slapped me.

"Why the fuck did you come out here?"

Somehow we ended up in the kitchen, and I grabbed a knife. This was the first time I had ever picked up a weapon while we were fighting. I was yelling and screaming, telling him to leave me alone. He was yelling and screaming, telling me to get out.

He grabbed me, and somehow I slit his leg with the knife. We both looked at each other and knew this whole scene was desperately wrong. We separated, and he looked at me, and I looked at him—no words, nothing.

I walked out of the apartment.

Six months pregnant, cold, and with no money, I started the almost six-mile walk home. I do not remember how far I walked before Kelvin picked me up. He stopped his car on the side of the road and sat there. I walked over and got in. There were no words, nothing. He dropped me off at home. Sadly, it was just another night of our usual arguing and fighting. The next day he called to make sure I was OK, keeping us locked in an unhealthy cycle of "I'm sorry," fighting, and violence.

CHAPTER 8

Pregnant and Unstable

There I was—nine months pregnant and calling Kelvin yet again to find out where he was. He hadn't checked on me like he promised. He told me he was going to run an errand, and he had been gone all day. Even more mentally unstable than before, I grabbed the keys, jumped in the car, and took off in my parent's gold Buick Park Avenue. I did not think anything about the value of this car and went looking for Kelvin exactly where I knew I would find him: in the hood. I knew of a girl he liked and had messed around in that specific neighborhood. The rumor was he had been seeing her my entire pregnancy.

As I drove into the neighborhood, I saw his car parked in front of the girl's house. I pulled up and left my parents big, gold, expensive Buick in the middle of the street, in the hood, still running. It was a hot summer day in early June, and I strode toward Kelvin's yellow Camaro with purpose. His windows were down, and the T-tops were off, so I opened the door and began smashing the tape deck I bought him. Let me tell you how crazy my thought pattern was. I figured, since I paid for the tape deck, if he wanted to mess around, he did not need to listen to the music I paid for!

He came running out of the girl's house before long, yelling at me to get out of his car. A woman across the street screeched at me too.

"Miss Jeffries! Miss Jeffries! What are you doing?"

With Kelvin grabbing and yelling at me, I totally ignored her, even when she said she'd call my parents. Somehow I got away from Kelvin and jumped back into my parent's car, which was still illegally parked in the middle of the street. I drove back to my quasi-suburban neighborhood and felt my heart sink to my stomach as I saw my parents standing outside waiting for me.

Honestly, if this were any other time, my parents would have "beat the hell out of me," or at least tried. (Once, they suggested I must be possessed by the devil since I would not listen to anyone.) Since I was pregnant, I got off easy.

"What the hell is wrong with you?" my mother asked. My parents are not ones to use profanity, but I now realize I brought that out of them.

"Give me the keys," followed up my father.

Upstairs in my bedroom, I cried all night.

Looking back on this story, I realize I could have been seriously injured, or worse, injured my unborn daughter. Learn from my mistakes and stand on what is righteous in life—what is good in life. We cannot allow our emotions to dictate who we are. If we can control our emotions, we can control our decisions. If we take the time to create an environment and an atmosphere of peace, we can be happy. If we create a life of thinking before we act, we can create an abundant life. When we sit in silence and listen to the Creator, He will help us make good decisions.

Delivery

My water broke on June 18, 1982, while I was outside sweeping the grass my dad had just cut. At first, I did not know that it had happened. I was eighteen, and I had no idea what that was supposed to look or feel like. I just remember my panties kept getting wet while I was sweeping, and I changed them at least three times before they stopped getting soaked.

The next day, a Saturday, I woke up and walked downstairs to see my mom in the living room.

"Mama, my stomach hurts."

With just one look at me, she knew what was wrong.

"Shelly you're in labor," she said as calmly as a summer breeze. "Go upstairs get your things, and let's go to the hospital."

A month earlier, my mom packed an overnight bag for the upcoming hospital visit. We all climbed into the same gold Buick Park Avenue I snuck off with a few weeks prior and headed to the hospital. I was only in labor for four hours, and my mom held my hand gently through all of it.

I looked at her and said, "Ma, it hurts."

With the same compassionate calm as before, she replied "I know Shelly but you'll be OK."

Right at that moment, the doctors came into my room. My mom looked at the doctors and said, "Please give her a shot. I don't want my daughter in pain." Soon after the epidural was administered, my daughter Audrei was born.

When it came time to complete the necessary paperwork, I still felt warm and happy from giving birth. But moments into the process, Kelvin and I once again got into an argument. What was so important that we had to argue about it the day our daughter was born? Not a clue. I just remember how I felt. I was so tired of arguing and fighting.

Reflection

It's easy, looking back, to see the warning signs that were missed. Please stop and reflect on what someone is telling you about your life that could save you, ease your pain, or help you create a life of peace. If they are right, listen.

Life Shift: Our Daughter Is Home

On the very first day I was home with Audrei, Kelvin came over to see her. We were upstairs, in the middle bedroom of my parent's home, and I was sitting on the bed, holding Audrei. When Kelvin arrived, we once again got into an argument. Within a few minutes, he hauled off and slapped me in my face.

The sound of smacking skin was so loud that my mother came running to my room. When she asked what had happened, I brushed her off.

"It's nothing, Ma. I'm OK."

Kelvin did not say a word. He just looked at me and left.

"Shelly," my mother said, leering at me with concerned eyes. "You can no longer live in this house. I have to raise two other girls, and I cannot allow them to see this going on. You have to move."

By the end of the month, my parents had moved me five blocks up the street to a high-rise apartment building. There was an option to reduce the rent for individuals with subsidized income, and I remember my mom broaching the subject of welfare with my dad.

"She's going to need some type of assistance. It's not just her. There's a baby now too."

"I don't want her on any assistance." My dad's rebuttals were always straightforward and to the point.

"Well, Freddie as she called my dad's given name, she needs it, and we have already put in an application."

My father walked away. Even though he didn't want it, I received food stamps and assistance for rent. I was in college at Davis Business College, working toward my degree in executive secretarial science and keeping the promise I made to my parents. Meanwhile, I worked in the office to make ends meet. Within a month of moving out of my parent's home, Kelvin and I started living together. I was eighteen years old, he was twenty, and we were raising our daughter.

Pictures from Kelvin and my apartment 1982

CHAPTER 9

The Sadness of Christmas

Kelvin and I lived together from June until December 1982, and I thought everything was going really well. We would visit our parents with our daughter. We would go on walks with her. He had his job at Kroger, and I had my education at Davis Business College. I would clean my parent's house, and they would pay me cash for extra pocket money, which Kelvin and I often used to eat at our favorite place at the time, Arby's.

On Christmas Day, Kelvin, six-month-old Audrei, and I watched TV and hung out at the house. I remember Kelvin picking Audrei up over his head and saying to her, "You're going to be my only child."

"Don't say that," I said, lightly tapping Kelvin's arm. "We will have more."

Kelvin just looked at me with a loving smile as he brought Audrei down from above his head, kissed her, and held her close to his chest. We just looked at her together. No words. Just quietness at what he had just said. We sat side by side in love and loving on our daughter. It was a calm that I felt from Kelvin, a peace and surety that he had completed his assignment on earth.

We had planned to attend a party later that evening. Maybe we shouldn't have. That Christmas, something went drastically wrong in our relationship.

The party on Secor Street in Toledo was a huge event that quite a few of our friends attended. Most of the people he grew up with were there too. But although we went to the party together, lived together, and had a daughter together, somehow Kelvin ended up leaving with another girl.

As if to comfort me in this absurd situation, one of his friends came over and told me, "Don't worry. I will take you home."

I was having none of it.

"I'm not going home," I said. "If he can leave me here, then I'm not going home."

I did not go home that night, and it was probably the worst decision I could have made. Everything escalated into an even worse situation that changed everyone's lives forever. That night, I stayed at a friend's house, and they took me home the next morning. Kelvin was already back at the apartment and had picked up Audrei from his parents' home. "Where have you been?" Kelvin asked as if I was in the wrong.

I ignored him.

"Where the fuck have you been?" he pressed on.

He stood tall and made it impossible to move past him.

"You left me!" I yelled back. "Look, I don't want to argue with you. You just tell me where you—"

SLAP! Kelvin hit me in my face. Hard.

I hit the ground hard and thought, this guy is crazy out of his mind. As I pulled myself up with both hands on the wall, Kelvin went to the room where Audrei was sleeping. Before I could get any words out, he was back and sent me to the floor again.

When we fought before, I would have been swinging back and trying to get my licks in. This time I did not even try. I knew I would lose. I always did. And I was just so tired. I just cried, asking him, "Let's just stop fighting. Please, let's stop fighting."

I was just so tired of it.

He kept yelling. "Don't you ever disrespect me that way! Don't you ever treat me that way in front of my friends again!"

I just wanted to get out of the apartment. Crawling, I slowly moved to the front door. Before I could get there, Kelvin walked over and kicked me twice in the stomach.

But I kept crawling.

When I reached the front door, I grabbed the handle, opened the door, and ran out. I ran as fast as I could down three flights of steps and went straight to my cousin's house.

I banged on the door desperately until my cousin answered. Tears streamed down my face.

"Michelle, are you OK?" she asked. "Are you OK?" "Yes, I'm OK" I said through my tears. "Kelvin and I were just fighting."

"Do you want me to call the police?" "No, please no. Just let me stay here for a while."

And I stayed until I was ready to go home.

CHAPTER 10

The Calm before the Storm

The day after Christmas, I went back to the apartment. I knew Kelvin was gone and had taken Audrei to his parents, Memia and Granddaddy. He called the apartment to make sure I was back and told me he would bring Audrei home early in the afternoon.

This seemed reasonable to me—we had to at least be civil about caring for our daughter. But while handing Audrei over to me, Kelvin and I argued, and he hit me yet again. With my daughter in hand, I ran into the kitchen and grabbed a knife. I started screaming.

"Get out! Get out!

"I'm not going anywhere!" he spat back. "This is my house!"

"Get out! Get out before I call the police!"

That threat shook him. I even grabbed the phone and actually dialed 911. I thought I had hung up before anyone answered, but shortly after Kelvin left, two male police officers came to our back door. The two men, one black and one white, proceeded to ask me questions.

"We received a 911 phone call," the black officer said.

"Yes, yes, that was me," I replied, my daughter on my hip.

"Is everything OK? Is there anything that we can do?" The black officer asked.

"No, my boyfriend and I just got in a fight again, and I'm just tired of it."

"Well, ma'am," the black officer continued. "If you press charges, we can arrest him, put him in jail overnight, allow him to cool off, and have him think about what's going on."

I was surprised by the offer, and even more shocked by how against the idea I felt. "I can't do that! That's my baby's daddy!"

I will never forget the look that the police officers gave each other. My answer seemed expected, and their glance at each other said, in a matter-of-fact way, "We are going to get a call back to this house."

The black police officer looked back at me and shook his head. "Well, ma'am, I understand that, but we're familiar with these situations, and if you allow us to pick him up, I'm sure it will be better for both of you."

I shook my head. "No. No, I can't do that."

The officer pulled a calling card out of his left pocket and handed it to me.

"If you need our help, please give us a call."

"Thank you," I said and shut the door.

Reflection

Do you remember when we talked about being silent and listening to determine the decisions you need to make in life? This was one of those times. I regret not making the decision to allow the officers to pick up Kelvin for the night. I wish I would have known to be silent and to listen. But because I didn't do either, the most unimaginable thing happened that night, and it would change the lives of everyone involved forever.

CHAPTER 11

The Storm

It was around 9:00 p.m. on the day after Christmas. Kelvin and his friend came back to the house, and they had been drinking. Although Kelvin wasn't much of a drinker, he was clearly drunk this night. Immediately after the door opened to our apartment, he started cursing and yelling at me. Already thrown off by the fact that he was drunk, I felt especially tired and overwhelmed by all the arguing and the fighting. I just wanted it to stop.

Everyone that knew us came up the three flights of steps through the back door into the kitchen area. The apartment just flowed better that way. When Kelvin came through the back door, he walked straight into the dining room where it connected to the living room.

I stayed in the living room, keeping my distance, hoping the yelling and cursing would just stop. But he didn't stop. Before long, I was yelling and cursing back, telling him to leave, to please just leave.

The situation escalated quickly. Kelvin charged and swung a punch at me. I'd been punched several times before in our previous fights, but they never really phased me much. Tonight was different. After his massive swing, it took several moments to come to my senses. And when I did, I realized how scared I was.

I ran through the apartment, trying to stay away from him. I frantically grabbed our daughter and just kept yelling at him to get out. I even pleaded to his friend, "Please get him out of here!" But no one was listening, and the whole room swirled with chaos.

Kelvin came rushing. I knew he was going to hit me again, but I also knew there was no way he would hit me if it meant he might hurt our daughter. I lifted Audrei's small, six-month-old body in front of my face as a human shield. Yes, I know it sounds stupid, but at that point the entire situation felt surreal. Even as I write this, the world around me is moving in slow motion, just like it did the day after Christmas in 1982.

Holding up my daughter did not stop Kelvin. He threw a punch around our daughter's little body and coldcocked me in my face. My mind went blank, and I literally saw stars. I never lost my balance or fell to the ground, but I was shaken into a fog.

"Damn, man," I heard Kelvin's friend say through the fog in my head. "Why did you hit her so hard?"

Everything in slow motion, I saw the friend, his hands over his mouth and his eyes wide as if asking, "What is going on?"

I felt my senses returning to my body and knew I had to keep my daughter safe. I ran to the corner of the dining room and handed Audrei to Kelvin's friend.

My daughter was as safe as she could be in this situation, I darted to the kitchen to once again grab a knife and scare Kelvin out of the house. This was the third time I'd pulled a knife on Kelvin, and it would also be the last.

I thought holding a knife would stop him from hitting me, but instead it infuriated him more.

"Get out! Get out!" I screamed, backing up slowly. "Leave me alone!" Kelvin pressed forward at a steady pace, jabbing at me.

I backed out of the kitchen into the dining room, and then into the living room. I swung the knife to keep him away and kept yelling, "Get out! Get out!"

Both of us in the living room, there's nowhere left for me to go. We stare at each other, and then Kelvin makes his move. The world moves in slow motion and fades in and out of blackness as Kelvin lunges forward and pulls his arm back to punch me. Another flash of black, and I see Kelvin look

51

down at his chest. The scene is static now, and my eyes scan down his body to follow his gaze.

Then I saw it. The knife sticking out of Kelvin's chest. The knife going straight through Kelvin's heart. I looked at my hands. Empty. What had I done?

The room became super bright, as if fireworks had been set off inside. The world sped up, keeping pace with my racing heart.

Kelvin fell back on the floor. He started yelling, "Take it out! Take it out!"

"Don't die! Don't die!" was all I could think to say.

He tried to pull the knife out but couldn't. I went over and tried.

"The knife is not coming out!" I yelled, "I got to call 911!"

I ran and called 911, then his parents.

When they picked up, I screamed hysterically through the phone. "I just stabbed Kelvin! I just stabbed Kelvin!"

My call to my own parents was just as frantic.

I didn't know what to do. The room was spinning, and I took off to the back door. I had no idea where I was going—I just had to get out.

I ran through the dining room, past his friend who was still holding Audrei, out the kitchen, and down the three flights of steps. I started running down the long driveway away from the apartment building, and by the time I got to the end of it, I could see my brother, the oldest of my siblings, running toward me. He must have run five blocks to get to me.

"Are you OK?" "Are you OK?"

"Yes!" I answered, but unsure if I was. "He's in there! He's in there!" I pointed toward the apartment, and my brother took off running into the apartment.

I only remember bits and pieces after that.

I remember being handcuffed and put in the back of the ambulance. Yes, the ambulance. They arrested me, but I remember someone saying, "She is in shock. We have to take her to the hospital." I remember being at the hospital. Once there, they checked my eyes to see if they were dilated. I never said a word; I just remember thinking, I'm in a nightmare. I have to be in a nightmare.

After I was cleared at the hospital, I was taken to the police station, where I was fingerprinted and had my picture taken. I asked if Kelvin was OK, and I can still hear the response in my head.

"He did not make it. He was dead on arrival." I don't even know who delivered the news.

I was put in a common area in the middle of the jail. Single cells lined the room, and inside were a bed and a toilet. My parents came to visit me early in the morning, Monday, December 27, 1982. They told me that everything was going to be OK.

I was able to go home that evening, but my mind was shattered by what had happened. The next day was no better. I can still feel the numbness of my mind. I learned from my mother that the worst event in your life is never something you get over. All you can do is learn to live with it.

When I came home from jail, I never went back to the apartment. To this day, I do not know who helped, but literally every single piece of my furniture was moved out of it and into my parents' home, where I stayed.

Reflection

My brother was a police officer at this time, and he was killed two years later by a drunk driver in September 1984. For years, I felt guilty over his death, that if I was a better person, he would never have died. That night with Kelvin and the knife changed me. I dealt with guilt, shame, and a sense of unforgiveness for almost thirty-seven years because of it. But no more! I am not going to let this define who I am. I now know and believe it is my responsibility to help others by telling my story. I cannot care what others think about me. I do not want to cause any new pain to anyone involved, but there are people hurting and in trouble, and this story can and will help bring them out! Why? Because of God's redemptive power. I have been redeemed by the blood of Jesus, and we all can be redeemed. We just have to speak, and God will do the rest.

As written in Isaiah 58:1–2: (The Voice)

> Tell My people about their wrongdoing; shout with a voice like
> a trumpet; Hold nothing back: say this people of Jacob's line and

heritage have failed to do what is right. And yet they look for Me every day. They pretend to want to learn what I teach, As if they are indeed a nation good and true, as if they hadn't really turned their backs on My directives. They even ask Me, as though they care, about what I want them to be and do, as if they really want Me in their lives.

Trust me. You really want God and His Word in your life. It is a serious game changer.

In Loving Memory—My brother Errol Vincent Jeffries (RIH—September, 1984)

Man Stabbed, Killed; Woman Is Charged

A Toledo man was killed late Sunday when he was stabbed in the chest during a quarrel in an apartment at 2129 Collingwood Blvd.

Police said Kelvin Spears, 20, of 3916 Inverness Ave., was taken to Mercy Hospital, where he was pronounced dead shortly after the stabbing about 11:30 p.m.

A woman identified as the victim's ~~[name]~~ of 0 Collingwood address, was treated at St. Vincent Hospital then taken to the Lucas County jail, where she was charged with murder pending arraignment today in Toledo Municipal Court.

A weapon was confiscated at the hospital, police said.

Kelvin Spears

Services for Kelvin Spears, 20, of 3916 Inverness Ave., who died Sunday in Mercy Hospital, will be at 1 p.m. Friday in Union Grove Baptist Church. He was a cashier two years at Foodtown Stores. Surviving are his daughter, Audrie; parents, the Rev. and Mrs. Jesse Spears; brother, Melvin Spears; sisters, Glenda and Gale Spears, and grandparents, Mrs. Delia Spears and Mrs. Corine Shuler. The body will be in the Dale Mortuary from 1 to 4 p.m. Thursday, when it will be taken to the church for wake services at 7.

Toledo Blade, 1982. My name is crossed out because my records are expunged.

CHAPTER 12

Mentally Fighting For My Life

Although I was still a student at Davis Business College, there was no way I could go to school the day after being released from jail. I woke up as usual to go to school, but it was immediately obvious class was not an option. And my mom agreed—but only that one time.

The next day, my mom came into my room.

"How are you, Shelly?"

"I'm good, Mama. But, Ma, I can't go to class. I just can't do it."

All of a sudden, my mom burst to life as if possessed.

"You have to go to class!" she exclaimed. "It's not about you! It's about that baby. You have to take care of her. Now get yourself together!"

I just stood there speechless. To turn around and go back into the world, just like that? How could she say that? What was going on?

I thought my mother had lost her mind and had absolutely no feelings. Of course, that wasn't true. My dad later told me that my mom immediately went into her bedroom and cried after that. She just knew what was best for me, even if it hurt to say it. My mother is one of the strongest women I know. I get my strength from her, and I feel stronger by telling this story and helping others see that life is all about giving God the glory. God was moving in my mother that day.

What happened that night with Kelvin has been the Achilles' heel of my life—the thorn in my side, the apple that Eve gave Adam. And only three days after it happened, all those feelings—the confusion, the sadness, the guilt—all of them were so raw. But I did as my mother told me and went to school.

I was called into the office by the granddaughter of the college's founder. Ms. Davis was an older woman with a black dress and black hair, and she had pale, white skin. She sat behind a huge wooden desk, and I walked in and took a seat.

"How are you?" she asked.

"I'm good. How are you?" I replied courteously.

Her hands were curled into a single fist-like mass at the center of her desk. "We heard what happened to you over the weekend." she said.

She was looking directly at me, and I stared back, hoping not to scream out of my skull.

"We know what happened was an accident, and we want to continue to support you. We want you to continue to work in the office, and we want you to continue your studies. We are here to help."

Tears rolled down my face like spring rain on a window. It was obvious that Miss Davis was not an emotional person, but the warm, small nod of approval she gave after I thanked her warmed my heart. I went to class and went to the office to work until it was time to go home.

The kindness shown by the entire staff at Davis Business College will never be forgotten.

Reflection

Throughout my story, I have shared with you that God has always been with me. Moreover, God, or your higher power, is always with you. We fail to see the help, because we only focus on what we can see. See your help today. "The angel of the Lord camps around those who fear Him, and delivers them" (Psalms 34:7).

Seeking Help

When trauma happens, that moment in time will stick with you forever. But you don't have to face your trauma alone. My parents' love, belief, and support started me on my journey toward getting through everything I had to endure. Because of them, I've learned how important it is for a light to illuminate the way forward immediately after coming out of a traumatic experience.

This light may shine through different means. The first is through love. For me, it was the moral characteristics of my parents' love that brought me guidance and support. Wherever the love in your life comes from, accept it. You will need it.

Second, light shines through the Word of God. Although my parents did not know to call someone to place me in therapy, I appreciate that they went one step better. They called Heleen Bond, a friend of my mom's, to champion my recovery. Aunt Heleen has transitioned to Heaven but left me with a tool I still utilize today: church. When she drove me to her church for the first time, I couldn't remember the last time I'd gone. I couldn't even remember the name of the church I'd last attended.

On my first visit, I accepted Christ as my personal Savior (as an adult) and began to read the Word of God every single day.

The Word of God gave me strength. The Word of God gave me power. Most of all, the Word of God gave me the ability to really understand and know that God loved me. I felt assured that God knew what I'd been through and that he'd known it would happen the moment He created the world. I felt the Word of God wrap around me like a warm blanket.

What had happened was a mistake. It was an accident. I did not mean for it to happen. I felt in my heart the need to just keep living. Those positive thoughts—I just had to keep saying them. They helped me remember that God is with me. He is with all of us.

CHAPTER 13

Love and Forgiveness
at a Funeral

A blessing undeserved. God is always using people to show His grace and mercy. He moved in the midst of this extremely unfortunate accident and used the love and forgiveness of Kelvin's family to show our community how mighty He is.

Kelvin died December 26, 1982, by my hand. Accident or not, it was my fault. It took almost an entire lifetime for me to say those words without crying or feeling guilt or shame. But it should not have taken so many years to let go of that pain, because the Spears family, with their incredible capacity for forgiveness, did not treat me any differently.

Reverend Spears and Mrs. Spears forgave and loved me immediately. I heard that when my parents walked in at Kelvin's funeral, which I did not attend,, everyone glared their way. There were even murmurs about fighting and hurting me. But amid the whispers and the stares, Reverend Spears, a tall, dark-skinned, handsome man with green eyes, stood up and said, "We love Michelle. We know it was an accident, and we don't want anything to happen to her." Reverend Spears' words changed the entire atmosphere of the funeral. They changed our community and my life.

I was and am so grateful for the true love and forgiveness Reverend Spears, Mrs. Spears, and their family have given me.

Reflection

There is nothing else to add. I will always love and forgive because God gave both love and forgiveness so freely through the Spears family.

1 John 4:19-21 We love because he first loved us. Whoever claims to love God yet hates a brother or sister is a liar. For whoever does not love their brother and sister, whom they have seen, cannot love God, whom they have not seen. And he has given us this command: Anyone who loves God must also love their brother and sister.

The Spears Family – This picture was taken February, 2017.
The adults in this picture were directly affected in 1982.

I asked God to give me a sign if He wanted me to write this book. Since I love pictures, I asked for a picture of everyone from 1982. He gave me that and more…the twins Kelvin's legacy.

The Shift Just Got Real

A life had been lost. By law, an investigation had to be completed to find out what happened. Although the Spears family did not press charges, the State of Ohio did.

We met with our lawyer, Jon Richardson. I remember sitting behind my parents as they talked with Mr. Richardson, who was sitting at his desk facing my parents. I sat in a third chair behind my parents.

"There is no way that your daughter can file or plead not guilty due to self-defense," Mr. Richardson told us. "She and the deceased had a history of fighting for the past four years."

While he was talking, he picked up a folder filled with papers as if to say, "Here is the proof."

"And because of that history, it would be best if we plead involuntary manslaughter, which simply means that it was an accident. It was not meant to be, but it definitely still happened."

I felt numb and didn't know what to think, if I was even thinking at all.

"She would receive thirty days in jail, three years of probation, and be released. Then she can go on and live the rest of her life."

We didn't seem to be left with any other option, but as I think back, the promise he made rings a bit hollow. After what I'd experienced, I could never just go on and live the rest of my life. I still shake my head when thinking about Mr. Richardson's comments… "She can go on and live the rest of her life." I had to accept my new reality.

The Plea

I went to court three times. My sister Sharon was a police officer (now a retired sergeant), and she would get off work and enter the courtroom wearing her uniform to support me and my parents. On the last day of court, Mr. Richardson told the courts I would take a plea. The judge agreed to the terms he had outlined, and I would be placed in jail in the summer of 1983.

Time for Jail

It was a beautiful, bright Sunday morning. I woke up, on the one hand, excited because it was Sunday, June 19, 1983—Father's Day and Audrei's first birthday. On the other hand, I was sad because I had to report the day after to the Lucas County Court System to be transported to Marysville Holding Prison.

We had a wonderful party for Audrei. She wore a beautiful blue-and-white dress, and we took the most adorable pictures of her in front of blooming roses next to the bricks on the side of my parents' home.

Reflection

I love youth. I love youth because, at eighteen years old, I did not completely understand the significance of leaving my child. All I knew was Audrei was safe and happy. I knew we were both protected by the love and care of my mom and dad. This thought truly brings tears to my eyes and heart. My life really was incredibly simple as a youth. Life was generally care-free because my parents took that burden off me.

I am so grateful for the parents God gave me. Looking back at how valuable their support was for me, I want to lighten the load of others going through a rough patch. I will always better myself by serving others, and we all need an advocate on Earth.

Monday, June 20, 1983

My parents drove me downtown to report in. I remember being scared and crying most of the trip there. At that time in my life, my mom was the one who would hit first as a means of punishment and ask questions later. Daddy, however, would always pour a glass of Hennessey with about three cubes of ice and have a two-hour conversation with you. When we got out of the car, my dad held my hands and said comforting words, as he always had. "Act like you are on vacation."

I looked into his eyes, and he smiled and nodded. That was all I needed to believe things would turn out OK. In a world of naysayers, what my daddy thought was enough for me.

Riding in the police van, it took a little over an hour to reach the holding prison. The building looked like a long white, one-story schoolhouse. I walked into the front door and up to a window to check into my new home.

Right next to the window was a set of doors. Beyond that set of doors to the left was a big recreation room or the common area. Beyond the same doors to the right were the bathrooms, showers, and laundry area. Straight ahead through the same doors were the the sleeping accommodations, a large room with beds lining both sides. Before entering the sleeping quarters and being introduced to my new bed, the guard led me past the large common area where twenty to thirty women lounged. Some sat on the large window ledges, others at tables, and some were standing around talking.

I put my things away and was escorted to the common area. Some of the women there immediately recognized me. Because my parents were well-known educators in the Toledo public school system, what had occurred between Kelvin and I was big news in our community. The women I knew told stories about how my parents were rich and that my parents would get me out early. Some told stories about what I had accomplished in high school. Those that didn't know me didn't care. What they cared about was getting close to me. Some of them made it very clear that if I did not conform, they would make me.

I learned quickly in jail that everyone needs someone to protect them.

Her name was DeAnna. She was an extremely attractive light-skinned, muscular woman. She wore a short afro, had a mustache and goatee, and was bowlegged. As I sat by myself, I looked up and saw her standing in front of me with her prison dress uniform. How DeAnna became bold and fearless enough to wear a dress in prison I'll never know.

"You need protection," she said matter-of-factly

"Protection?"

"Yes, I can protect you."

I looked around the room and saw the other women watching us. I did not know what else to do. I nodded my head, and for the next thirty days, I was considered DeAnna's girlfriend. It was apparent that no one was going to challenge her. Only once did someone approach me when DeAnna was not around and told me, "Your ass is mine when we get to the farm. Your bitch can't protect you there." The farm was the main prison we would go to after leaving the holding facility.

I never told DeAnna what the woman said. I had enough just keeping my thoughts straight on a daily basis. I did not need outside drama. Plus, I prayed I'd never have to go to the farm, but if I had to go there, I wanted there to be as few issues as possible.

God Favored Me

On my fourth day in prison, a job posting for a laundry tenant was tacked on the information board. Without hesitation, I applied for the job. The guards even held interviews (though they were in the cafeteria). Out of the four inmates they interviewed, I got the position. When I think back on this story, I can't help but say to myself, "Girl, you even volunteered in prison!

I received one phone call per week, and I used my first one to call my parents the day after I was hired for the laundry tenant position. My daddy was so cool about it.

"Yeah, keep your head up and stay busy. Remember, you are on vacation and will be home in thirty days." I still shake my head joyfully at the brilliance of these words. What a way to motivate an eighteen-year-old that is unsure and unstable! It worked. I stayed busy, and in thirty days, I was called to the office and told I would be going home.

Jail Is Real

As I shared with you, DeAnna was protecting me, but as you might guess, that came with strings attached. To this day, I believe nothing happened sexually between us simply because the facility was so cramped. One day, as I was coming out of the laundry area, DeAnna came in to use the bathroom. She stopped directly in front of me and began feeling me up and kissing me. I am not sure what would have happened if I made it to the farm. I am grateful I never had to find out. My point in sharing this story is that if you do not want to experience jail, don't do something that will get you there! I do my best to follow the rules and encourage others to do the same. That means school rules, church rules, marriage rules—all rules! As written in Romans 13:1–2 (New Living Translation),

> Everyone must submit to governing authorities. For all authority comes from God, and those in positions of authority have been placed there by God. So anyone who rebels against authority is rebelling against what God has instituted, and they will be punished.

Do I make mistakes? Absolutely! I am and probably will always be the person that goes to the edge and looks over the line to consider what would happen if I crossed it. At this point in my life, I just do my best to make sure that if I do cross a line, it hurts me more than it hurts others.

Audrei's first birthday

Audrei's fifth birthday on the bricks and in front of the roses

CHAPTER 15

An Opportunity

In September 1983, I was back at college finishing my courses. Looking back from my current perspective, life seemed normal; however, it was nothing but. It was difficult for me to go anywhere in my community because of the looks people gave me and the loud, overt comments made as I would walk by. It did not matter if I was at someone's house or at the mall— people would look, stop, stare, and point.

"Yeah, that's her. She killed someone."

If they knew me, they would even say Kelvin's name.

These comments stuck with me for a very long time. But it's my mother's words that got me through it.

"It's not about you. It's about that baby. You have to take care of her."

I was going to stay sane for my daughter. I had to. She needed me now more than ever.

In January 1984, I was pulled out of class by one of my teachers. I remember her name and how she looked. We even talked a few years back. Yet even after 37 years, I will never share her name in writing. For this story, let us call her Mrs. Reid.

Mrs. Reid walked me to a classroom at the corner of the building's large atrium. At this time, Davis College classrooms were partitioned off by accordion doors. We sat down at two desks facing each other.

"We have a job opportunity for you," she said. "General Motors in Sandusky, Ohio, is looking for minorities to hire for secretarial positions."

I had never heard of Sandusky.

"Would you be interested?"

This whole conversation was a true blessing. Davis Business College helped students find jobs after graduation. My answer was obvious.

"Yes, of course!"

"OK," she started. "They are going to have you complete an application. On the application there will be a box asking if you have ever been convicted of a felony."

She paused.

"Mark no."

I stared at her wide-eyed. "Mark no?"

She nodded. "Yes, mark no."

She and I both knew I had been convicted for involuntary manslaughter, at that point a Class 4 Felony. Surely there'd be consequences if I wasn't honest and checked yes rather than no. But could I afford to miss out on this opportunity when I had a daughter to care for? I left our conversation knowing I'd fill out an application, but I had no clue which box I'd fill.

CHAPTER 16

One Chance Is All You Need

Check The Box

I drove to Sandusky in January 1984 to fill out an application to work for General Motors. I remember how excited my parents were. They made the comment that if I was hired, I could further my college education, and the company would pay for it.

It was my mom's excitement and belief in me that provided the opportunity to attend Davis Business College. On a summer day, a congratulatory card came in the mail from the school. Shortly after, we set a date to meet with a guidance counselor. When the meeting came, the woman behind the desk handed me the card I supposedly completed to attend the college. I looked at the card, then I looked over at my mom and we both smiled. It was in my mom's handwriting. She knew all I needed was one chance. And so I started college in the fall of 1982. By 1984, I graduated with my associate's degree and knew people around me would always support me.

As I walked into General Motors, I was embracing another opportunity someone had put in front of me. If all went well, I'd be hired and start anew in Sandusky, Ohio. But I still had to make my choice about that little box on the application.

I walked in and met Althea Johnson, a black woman who remains one of my mentors and friends. She was so kind and offered to see her about anything if I was hired. I was escorted to the office of the hiring manager, Cecil Weatherspoon, a black man. I was happy to see African American faces in leadership positions. Mr. Weatherspoon provided the application, and I set forth in filling it out. Then came to the question: "Have you ever been convicted of a felony?" I saw both boxes. One box said yes, and the other box said no. As my hand hovered over the page, I heard Mrs. Reid's voice, "Mark no." In what felt like an out-of-body experience, I felt a force push my hand to mark no.

I turned in the application, completed the interview, and just like that, I got the job. I started on Monday, February 6, 1984, as a General Motors employee. I was nineteen years old, and Audrei was eighteen months. Since there was a ninety-day probation period before I became a full employee, my parents kept Audrei in Toledo for the first three months to ensure I'd make it to work every day.

Friends

It was a dark, emotional first year out of Toledo. If my BFF Tonya hadn't spent most of the year with me, I would have been lost. I was on legal probation and had to report downtown each month. Since no one in Sandusky knew me, I certainly did not want anyone's first impression of me connected to being an ex-felon. I began my journey of keeping this secret as close to me as possible. Despite the fact of wanting to keep my secret, if I became friends with you, I told you my story immediately. I would allow you to decide whether you wanted to remain friends with me. I want to recognize a few that have stuck with me as A1's since day one Brenda Jones, Brigitte Green-Churchwell, and Danny Aaron, Jr. There are so many more friends in Sandusky that I now call family, but these folks have been there for me since the beginning. Thanks, guys! I appreciate you!

I worked for General Motors for thirty-two years before being permanently laid off in November 2015. Before the plant closed, it was an amazing place to work. Everyone always wondered why I was so happy all the time. But the answer was simple. Life had given me another chance—the one chance I needed to start afresh. General Motors paid for my undergrad and graduate degrees. I graduated with my master's degree in July 2007, less than a year before General Motors stopped its tuition assistance program. I had just made it! Thank you, Lord! "Trust in the Lord always, for the Lord God is the eternal Rock" (Isaiah 26:4).

Graduation Davis Business College 1984

Brenda Jones

Danny Aaron, Jr. and Vincent

Bridgette Green Churchwell

CHAPTER 17

God's Angel on Earth Handpicked for Me

I had seen Vincent many times. He was an engineer at General Motors and worked in the testing lab. Everyone had to go through this department in order to get to the salaried area of the building. We would speak every morning, and he was always very kind. Plus, he had an amazing body.

One day in August 1986, I was having an emotional moment and really just needed to talk to someone. I walked down to the lab and started telling Vincent everything about me. I told him the good, the bad, the ugly and the very ugly. I told him about my past, about what happened with Kelvin, and about my family. He just listened and never judged me. He never asked questions but became one of my best friends.

Our First Date

In March 1987, Vincent asked me out on a date. Why would he want to go on a date with me? He knew all my secrets, all the dark areas of my life. Yet he asked, and I told him yes. I asked my parents to come to Sandusky to babysit Audrei, and together Vincent and I went to Playhouse Square in Cleveland to see *Cats*.

The night of our date, my parents came to my apartment, and I introduced them to Vincent. My mother and father went through the usual questions with Vincent: "What do you do?" and "Where do you work?" When he told them he was an engineer at GM, the light that went off in my mother's eyes was priceless.

"Oh, engineer," she said, mouth agape. Oh my—"

Before she could make another statement or ask another question, I pushed Vincent to the door and right out of the apartment.

"Let's go!" I said, knowing my parents were about to interrogate him. Vincent and I still laugh about that story.

A Father's Wisdom

The next weekend, I went to my parent's home and sat on the screened porch with my dad.

"I like that Vincent," he said.

"Daddy, you don't even know him."

"Well, he seems to be a really nice guy."

"Daddy, he is not my type. He is not even just a nerd. He is a super nerd."

My dad smiled and in his cool calm voice said, "I like him. I think you should learn to like him."

My daddy got up, walked back into the house with a smile on his face as if to say, "I said what I said. Now let's see if you are going to listen."

I've told you many stories about my past, and in most of them, I didn't listen to my father. But at this point, I was twenty-two, and I had seen the consequences of not heeding his advice. As he walked away, I said to myself, "I'm going to listen this time and see what he sees."

Vincent and I started dating, and my dad was right. I fell in love with Vincent's mind and so much more. He was one of the smartest men I had ever met. Even when he used big words, he made them simple for me to understand. At this time, I had not obtained my bachelor's or my master's degrees. I had so many skeletons and secrets that I lacked self-confidence and had very low self-esteem. I couldn't understand why a man of his caliber, an engineer and graduate of Northwestern University, would date someone like me. I once asked him that specific question, and he said, "I met your family, and I know that you have potential."

Potential. I am not sure if I have yet reached the potential Vincent saw in me. But one thing is for certain: I will strive and improve every day and be the godly woman that God gave to this godly man almost thirty-two years ago.

June 1987

It was June 1987, and Vincent and I attended a friend's wedding in Michigan. Vincent was in the wedding party, which meant he was paired with a bridesmaid and had to walk her into the reception and do a dance with her. However, being young and inexperienced with wedding protocol, I thought that Vincent had ditched me for this other chick. Worse, I knew Vincent had dated this girl prior to me. The old Michelle came out in fighting form.

I ended up telling our friends what was going on, and they encouraged me to drink five different types of drinks to calm down. This included a shot, wine, and mixed alcohol. After the fifth drink, I was more than drunk and found the courage to go out on the dance floor and confront Vincent about the girl he was dancing with. I embarrassed both of us. Vincent took me by the arm and said, "Let's go." No other words were said until we reached the car, where he told me we were leaving.

While we were driving back to the hotel so he could pack up and take me home, I cursed at Vincent and spit in his face. Again with no words said, Vincent pulled off the expressway, pulled up to a hotel (not ours), got out of his car, came around and opened my door and said, "Get out." That sobered me right up! I got out of the car, not knowing what was going to happen next. He closed my door, got back in the driver's seat, and drove away.

I could not believe what was happening.

Fortunately, we had friends that were at the hotel, Kevin and Inga Reeves. I called them, and they came and picked me up. Kevin fussed at me the entire time and asked me why I even got out of the car. Inga just smiled as Kevin fussed.

"They're going to get married." In her New Jersey accent voice.

"Married!" Kevin screamed. "I would never marry her crazy behind!"

While writing this book, my dear friend Kevin Reeves passed away after battling pancreatic cancer. I love you and miss you, Kevin, and I will always share this story with the world about how you rescued me (well Inga–lol) and made sure I got home safely.

The day after my drunken incident, a Sunday, my parents were in the kitchen eating breakfast. I walked in and my dad told me that Vincent had called him and told him that he left me on the expressway in Michigan.

"You know what I told him?" he asked me. "I said, 'Good, let her find her own way home.'"

I could not believe my dad was on Vincent's side. I am tickled to say both of my parents are still on Vincent's side today.

Vincent had a test the next day on Monday. He was working on his master's degree and needed to study. Nevertheless, I called him repeatedly until he answered the phone.

"You need Jesus," he said.

No one had ever said that to me the way that he said it. It took me all the way back to my youth and reminded me that I had stopped moving forward on my walk with Jesus.

New Beginnings

That Friday, I went to church with Tonya. I received the anointing of the Holy Ghost and began to speak in tongues. That was the beginning of my true, sincere walk with God.

The next weekend, I visited Granddaddy, and asked if I could come back home to his church. "Baby, you are always welcome home," he said. I started attending church with Granddaddy and the Spears family.

The next Friday, Vincent called me and told me that he too had been filled with the Holy Ghost. Moreover, our relationship started over with Christ as our foundation. He, too, joined Granddaddy's church, and we attended together for close to twenty years.

In August, only five months after we started dating, Vincent asked me to marry him. Reverend Jesse L. Spears married us the following year, on June 4, 1988.

"The man who finds a wife finds a treasure, and he receives favor from the Lord" (*Proverbs 18:22 [NLT]*).

The Wedding

CHAPTER 18

Last Thoughts

My records are expunged, so I do not have to tell this story; however, I do so because I see so many women, young and old, going through situations similar to mine. I see them suffering from low self-esteem, a lack of confidence, unforgiveness, and shame and guilt from mistakes they made. I talk to many women trying to get out of a broken relationship they think is full of love.

For years, I was not in prison, and my records were expunged, but I still felt as though I was in a cage. I do not feel that way anymore. My mind, body, and soul are free. Now it is time for me to help you walk in your freedom and live your authentic truth. I've shared my story, and here are the lessons I hope you can take from it.

Lessons Learned

1. Using your voice to share your most difficult experiences with others is the most freeing experience you'll ever have.
2. One story, one moment, one decision, does not define your success or your failure.
3. If you are in a bad relationship, get out and get help!

4. Making any decision, "It is simple, but rarely is it easy. You have to do the work.

5. Do not be afraid to face your past. The only thing that can hurt you is the fear you do not release. Let go of your fear of the past. You are holding it; it's not holding you.

6. Make better decisions by looking at others who have gone through similar situations.

7. Guilt is like plaque on your teeth. If you do not let go of guilt, you will decay from the inside out.

8. Shame keeps you living a small life in the shadows of the world.

9. Unforgiveness will eliminate the kindness or compassion you have for yourself and others. *Accept* the awful thing that happened in your life, *acknowledge* what happened, then *let go.* Learn to forgive yourself and others. Do not bombard your mind with the question of why bad things happen. When you try to figure out why something happened to you, you attack yourself repeatedly with the same pain. *Stop. Let go and live!*

10. "The thief cometh not, but for to steal, to kill, and to destroy: I am come that they might have life, and that they might have it more abundantly" (John 10:10).

11. Stop allowing the world and all that is wrong in it to steal your mind, kill your joy, and—when you have no strength to fight—destroy your life.

Homework Assignment:

Pray daily.
Read God's Word daily.
Love everyone.
Forgive frequently.

Final Tool: Talk with wise counsel. Never go on this journey called life alone.

* * *

Me and my dad, mom and sisters

Me, Vincent and our children and twin grand children

May, 2019—My Mom and Memia
the women that prayed for our family throughout these years.
Audrei and Peyton (my daughter and grand daughter).

CHAPTER 19

There is More

There are so many more stories, so many more facets of my life that I could share with you about how God was in every moment. But I only found God in those moments upon reflection, which is why it's important for you to do your homework. Because I did the homework, I now thrive. This does not mean that I do not have problems, but now my problems do not control my life.

I pray that the stories I've shared have been valuable for you. I pray you were inspired to continue your journey to a healthy, happy, abundant life.

Many different people make major impacts in our life journeys, and those influential people can coach each of us. I hope I have been that kind of light for you, but now it's up to you. *You have to put in the work!*

Along with a coach or counselor, you need a friend to help you through hard times. I cannot express how important this is. God saw fit to bless me with my husband, Vincent, and he has been my friend for almost thirty-four years. But we all have a friend who has been with us for our whole lives—Jesus. As Proverbs 18:24 reads, "A man of many companions may come to ruin, but there is a friend who sticks closer than a brother."

To connect with your new lifelong friend, Jesus, PFRM—pray, fast, read, meditate—and He will show up in your life every day with a smile, advice, no judgment, and so much more.

Thank you again for sharing this journey with me. I pray you now have the tools to move forward in taking life to the next level. Remember, as serious as your problem may be, if no one has died, it can be rectified. But with God, death does not mean the end of hope. If someone has died, God's redemptive power has justified forgiveness.

See you in my next book!

BOOK COVER

The Butterfly

Butterflies are deep and powerful representations of life. Many cultures associate the butterfly with our souls. The Christian religion sees the butterfly as a symbol of resurrection. Around the world, people view the butterfly as representing endurance, change, hope, and life.

The Color Turquoise

The color turquoise is associated with meanings of refreshing, feminine, calming, sophisticated, energy, wisdom, serenity, wholeness, creativity, emotional balance, good luck, spiritual grounding, friendship, love, joy, tranquility, patience, intuition.

ACKNOWLEDGEMENT OF APPRECIATION AND GRATITUDE

Thank you for joining me on this journey of true love and true forgiveness. If I have asked once, I have asked myself a thousand times, why write a book about my life? My life is not extraordinary. The decisions that I have made have not always been the best. All I know is that God called me to tell my story.

"My story." I now know that the story of Michelle's life is really God's story. So is yours, and so is everyone's. Trying to find the words to write in this book has been overwhelming. I now know that my life is not my own. I now know that as long as I focus on my spiritual being, the things of this world really do not upset me.

By telling this story—God's story—I have expressed Him in me for all of you. Realizing this was so real and so magnificent! After all I have gone through, I see now that God kept me to tell the story of my purpose. Moreover, in telling His story of my purpose, it is His intent that you read this book to find your purpose.

Because this book affects so many people in my personal life, I have to tell them thank you for allowing me to share it. Thank you for loving God.

It is the love you have for Him and the love you have for yourself that has allowed each of you to love others in spite of it all.

My Personal Life Lessons Learned

Find your inner purpose. Be true to God. Love with no strings attached.

Love God. Love yourself. That makes it so easy to love others.

Love is not a simple word, nor is it just a word calling for us to take action.

Love is submerging (metaphorically, of course) your entire being— your heart, mind, soul, spirit, and body— in the blood of Jesus that was shed over two thousand years ago. When you emerge all you will see is peace, joy, mercy, and connection. Love is compassion, and you will feel the compassion God has for each of us. There will be a desire and a yearning for yourself and others to live an abundant life.

This reminds me of the words Reverend Jesse L. Spears: "Our story needs to be on the Oprah Winfrey Show. It will show everyone that love and forgiveness can prevail."

Thanks, Granddaddy Spears. Because of your own forgiveness, you allowed God's righteousness to manifest in my life. You are a spiritual seed planter.

Thank you, Mom and Dad. You never, ever gave up on me!

Thank you to my oldest sister, Sharon, for always showing up and believing in me.

Thank you, Juilee and Treva, for watching me change from just the sister you knew loved you into the sister that loves and prays for you.

To my brother Errol (RIH): Thank you for always and forever watching over me.

To the Spears family: Reverend Jesse L. Spears, Mrs. Lillian Spears, Melvin, Glenda, and Gail. I am so sorry you had to endure such pain because of my actions; however, I am more thankful that God is using you to illuminate his true love and true forgiveness in such a great, great family. Thank you so much for your God-like love!

To all of my family and friends: Thank you for standing by me with continuous love and prayers.

To the Rhodes family: William Rhodes (RIH), Betty Rhodes, Dennis, Paul, Diane, and Michelle, when others would have said no, you said yes. Thank you!

To my beautiful daughter, Audrei: I have done my best to raise you in the way God wants you to go, and you succeeded. You did not make my mistakes. You listened to the God in me, and because of that, you have become a beautiful, godly woman and mother. God is going to reward you with blessings, and you will not have enough room to receive them all. Thank you for loving me!

To my son, Alan, my baby: When you were younger, you asked so many questions, many of which I did not want to answer. Here are some of the answers to how God has kept our family and protected us. Thank you, son, for your boldness. Now conquer the world through your teaching and compassionate heart! Thank you for loving me!

To my God-given soulmate, Vincent Alan (Boo) Rhodes: It has truly been a journey, and I would not have come out on top without you in my life. You are the epitome of Ephesians 5:25, "Husbands love your wives just as Christ loved the church and gave himself up for her." You have given me so much of you—so much love, guidance, compassion, patience, tolerance, peace, joy and all other positive, caring, from-the-heart adjectives in the universe! You are my rock, the solid foundation placed on this earth for such a time as this. Thank you for praying for our family for the past thirty-plus years. Thank you for being the best provider a family could ask for. Thank you for loving God, loving yourself, and loving others. Our future is brighter because He holds it in the palm of His hand. I praise God for our yesterdays, our union, our life, and our tomorrows. Most of all thank you for allowing me to hold on to my memories and love for Kelvin. His life mattered. His and my relationship mattered. Moreover, you shared in our memories with so much empathy. That gift is priceless.

ENDNOTES

Adjectives to describe your inner gifts

	agreeable	alert	alluring	amazing
ambitious	amusing	attentive	awesome	boundless
brave	bright	calm	capable	charming
cheerful	clever	coherent	comfortable	confident
conscientious	considerate	consistent	cooperative	courageous
creative	credible	cultured	dashing	dazzling
debonair	decisive	decorous	delightful	detailed
determined	diligent	discerning	discreet	dynamic
eager	eclectic	efficient	elated	eminent
enchanting	encouraging	endurable	energetic	enterprising
entertaining	enthusiastic	excellent	excited	exclusive

exuberant	*fabulous*	*fair*	*faithful*	*fantastic*
fearless	*fine*	*frank*	*friendly*	*funny*
generous	*gentle*	*glorious*	*good*	*groundbreaking*
happy	*hard-working*	*harmonious*	*helpful*	*hilarious*
honorable	*impartial*	*ingenious*	*insightful*	*inventive*
industrious	*inscrutable*	*instinctive*	*jolly*	*joyous*
kind	*kind-hearted*	*knowledgeable*	*level*	*likeable*
lively	*logical*	*lovely*	*loving*	*loyal*
lucky	*mature*	*meticulous*	*modern*	*multi-talented*
nice	*obedient*	*optimistic*	*organized*	*painstaking*
peaceful	*perceptive*	*perfect*	*persistent*	*placid*
plausible	*pleasant*	*plucky*	*productive*	*professional*
protective	*proud*	*punctual*	*quiet*	*receptive*
reflective	*reliable*	*relieved*	*resolute*	*responsible*
rhetorical	*righteous*	*robust*	*romantic*	*sedate*
seemly	*selective*	*self-assured*	*sensitive*	*sharp*
shrewd	*silly*	*sincere*	*skillful*	*smart*
smiling	*sophisticated*	*splendid*	*steadfast*	*stimulating*
strategic	*studious*	*successful*	*succinct*	*talented*
thoughtful	*thrifty*	*tough*	*trustworthy*	*unbiased*
unprecedented	*unusual*	*upbeat*	*vigorous*	*vivacious*
warm	*willing*	*wise*	*witty*	*wonderful*

Thank You for Reading My Book!

I really appreciate all of your feedback, and I love hearing what you have to say.

I need your input to make the next version of this book and my future books better.

Please leave me an honest review on Amazon letting me know what you thought of the book.

Thanks so much!

Michelle Jeffries Rhodes

ABOUT THE AUTHOR

Michelle Jeffries Rhodes is a keynote speaker, life coach, and counselor. With thirty-two years of experience in corporate leadership, Michelle utilizes her passion to help women create lives of peace and productivity.

She and her husband, Vincent, have two children, Audrei and Alan, and twin grandchildren, Peyton and Kelvin.

BONUS

To receive your FREE Shifting! Journal, visit
https://michellejeffriesrhodes.com/shifting-life-product
(shipping not included)

Thank you!
Michelle

Made in the USA
Middletown, DE
06 November 2023

41869339R00066